FIRST STEPS IN INTERVENTION WITH YOUR CHILD WITH AUTISM

FRAMEWORKS FOR COMMUNICATION

PHIL CHRISTIE,
ELIZABETH NEWSON,
WENDY PREVEZER
AND SUSIE CHANDLER

ILLUSTRATED BY PAMELA VENUS

JESSICA KINGSLEY PUBLISHERS
LONDON AND PHILADELPHIA

First published in 2009
by Jessica Kingsley Publishers
116 Pentonville Road
London N1 9JB, UK
and
400 Market Street, Suite 400
Philadelphia, PA 19106, USA

www.jkp.com

Library of Congress Cataloging in Publication Data

First steps in intervention with your child with autism : frameworks for communication/Phil Christie ... [et al.].

p. cm.

Includes bibliographical references and index.

ISBN 978-1-84905-011-1 (pb : alk. paper) 1. Autism in children--Popular works. 2. Children with disabilities--Means of communication. I. Christie, Phil.

RJ506.A9F575 2009

618.92'85882--dc22

2008050208

British Library Cataloguing in Publication Data

A CIP catalogue record for this book is available from the British Library

ISBN 978 1 84905 011 1

Printed and bound in the United States by
Thomson-Shore, 7300 Joy Road, Dexter, MI 48130

CONTENTS

1 INTRODUCTION

The material in this book was first produced as part of an action research project[1] carried out at the Early Years Diagnostic Centre in Nottingham (now re-named the Elizabeth Newson Centre). The project aimed to develop and evaluate a model of good practice linking early diagnosis and intervention, with a particular emphasis on early social communication. Both the diagnostic assessment and the intervention that followed were carried out as a partnership between parents and professionals.

The children involved in the project were aged under three years at the time of the initial assessment and the team were keen to produce guidelines for intervention that started by helping parents understand what autism meant in relation to their own child's development. This included an understanding of some of the differences in developmental pathways between a child with autism and a typically developing child.

The approach was based on work developed by the authors as researchers, clinicians and practitioners from their involvement at the University of Nottingham, Sutherland House School and the Early Years Diagnostic Centre (the specialist school and assessment service that are part of the provision made by the Nottingham Regional Society for Adults and Children with Autism, NORSACA, a parent-led charity based in Nottingham). Central to this approach is the view that one of the major difficulties for children with autism is in developing social empathy in the same way as other children. Typically developing children move steadily towards becoming competent communicators during their first year of life through their repeated interactions and dialogues with adults, through what are known as the 'pragmatics' of language. These pragmatics include body language (such as gesture, facial expression, eye-contact, posture and stance), listening skills, using intonation and volume, understanding intention, sharing understanding and turn-taking. Children with autism find it very difficult to take advantage of their social opportunities at a very early age because of the difficulties they have in making sense of these pragmatics, which are the building-blocks, or first steps, in developing communication. The approach outlined is aimed at helping parents play and interact with their child in such a way that intensifies the experience, and clarifies its meaning, so as to enable the child to become more effective in his or her communication.

The guidelines were written and re-written in the form of individual booklets, refined through experience and feedback from the families involved in the project. During the project families received weekly support from a member of the team who worked directly with the child and also discussed and modelled approaches with the family. Families also attended a ten-week course of weekly workshop sessions where they were able to learn more about the approach, discuss their individual child and share experiences with other families. The guidelines were first published by the Early Years Diagnostic Centre as a series of six illustrated booklets that parents could use in whichever order suited them and the stage of development their child had reached.

One of the central considerations of the project was to produce a model that was as close to 'real life' as possible. This meant maintaining the integrity of the approach, with its emphasis on interactive methods and prioritizing early social communication, but allowing sufficient flexibility so that families could adapt the methods to their own particular circumstances. In clinical and educational settings many parents had raised concerns with us about approaches that were too prescriptive in the way programmes were devised, and the level of intensity that was suggested. During the project each family kept a log of the time they spent playing or working with their child. While many set aside regular sessions for interactive play, most commented that they also incorporated the approach and ideas into some of their daily routine, such as bathtime or playing in the garden. As one parent said:

'We seem to capture the moment more, but also plan times with [him], and all think about how we can use different opportunities to help his communication.'

This quote came from one of the regular interviews that were part of the evaluation of the project. Families were asked in what ways they and their child had benefited and what they felt about the approach. Others said:

> *I know how to play with him now, I have lots more ideas. I know how to deal with his tantrums now and other things he does. It helps having more and more knowledge about autism, it helps me understand him and also what to do.*

> *It's given us the strength to cope with [him] and to work with him. It's taught us how to enjoy him.*

One mother simply commented: 'I now have a communicative child!'

Looking beyond the life of the research project, it was always the intention of the team to develop materials that could be of value to both parents and professionals. It was planned that the principles of the model could be adapted by other agencies and could be easily accommodated alongside the services available to the child and family, such as early years provision and speech and language therapy. Following the project a collaborative venture was set up in Nottinghamshire between NORSACA and Local Education and Health services to establish the Early Communication and Autism Partnership (ECAP), which is now available to children and families across the county of Nottinghamshire.

The book is designed to be used directly by parents looking to better understand their child and, in turn, to help to improve their child's understanding and communication. It can also be used by professionals working to support and enable families. The content is aimed at pre-school children at an early stage of communication, but many of the ideas can also be usefully applied to children of school age if they are at that stage of development.

Throughout the text we have used the male gender to refer to the child with autism to reflect the fact that there are more boys with the condition than girls.

We are grateful to The Baily Thomas Charitable Fund, which funded both the research and the initial publication of the material in this book.

NOTES

1. Chandler, S., Christie, P., Newson, E. and Prevezer, W. (2002) 'Developing a diagnostic and intervention package for 2– to 3-year-olds with autism. Outcomes of the Frameworks for Communication approach.' *Autism: The International Journal of Research and Practice 6*, 1, 47–69.

2

DEVELOPING AN UNDERSTANDING OF AUTISM

The aim of this chapter is to help improve your understanding of autism in general and what this means to your own child in particular. It serves as an introduction to the rest of the chapters, which go on to suggest some specific ways in which you can work with your child to help improve his communication, which is the foundation for all future learning and development.

Difficulty in developing *social empathy* (an understanding of other people's thoughts, emotions, behaviour and language) is central to the pattern of difficulties that go to make up autism. If the child has difficulties in empathizing with us then we, first of all, need to try to empathize with him. In order to do this effectively we need to try to imagine how the world must seem to him. We will do this more easily as we begin to understand autism and its effect on development.

Whenever possible, we need to diagnose autism as early as we can. This diagnosis should then act as a 'jumping off point', helping us to plan a highly individual programme, which aims to address some of the core difficulties that are shared by all children with autism. While it is crucial that we pay very close attention to the child's strengths, and value him as a unique individual, we can also learn from the contrasting ways that children with autism develop when compared with other children.

WHAT DOES A DIAGNOSIS OF AUTISM MEAN?

Autism as a 'spectrum disorder'

The severity of autism can vary greatly from one individual to another and the term 'autism spectrum' has been used as a way of describing this range in severity. At one end of the spectrum children can be very severely affected, while at the other their difficulties seem much less marked.

Autism is found in children of all levels of ability, from those who are above average in their intelligence to those who have severe learning difficulties. Sometimes those children who seem to be less severely affected, or show good levels of ability in some areas of development, are described as having Asperger syndrome or high functioning autism. Many children with a diagnosis of autism do have some degree of learning difficulty. It is, though, very hard to assess the intelligence of any particular young child who has this sort of social communication problem. For example, if we were to try to see if he could carry out a range of tasks that were designed to measure his intelligence, the fact that he didn't succeed with a certain activity might be because he didn't understand what we asked him, or because he wasn't able to pay attention or cooperate for long enough to enable him to do so. We can only really get a better understanding of his abilities and strengths by knowing what he does in lots of different settings, with different activities and over a longer period of time.

One thing that we can be certain about, though, is that whatever the extent of the autism (and any accompanying learning difficulties) may turn out to be, your child *can* make considerable progress. What will help most with this is his parents and the professionals involved understanding the nature of his abilities and difficulties better; working together to promote his understanding and communication.

Diagnosing autism

It has become fashionable, over recent years, to say that children shouldn't be 'labelled'. We feel very strongly that specific diagnosis is important as a starting point in helping everyone involved to understand a child; both his difficulties and his strengths. Indeed one person with autism has described the diagnosis as being a 'signpost'. A diagnosis should set out the defining criteria for that particular condition, as opposed to other possible ones. In doing so a 'differential diagnosis' is being made. For example, autism as opposed to another condition, such as specific language disorder. The diagnostic description should then go on to explain in considerable detail just how those criteria affect the development of *this* child as an individual.

Sometimes there is also a reluctance to diagnose a child early on and some professionals will say that 'you can't diagnose autism before three' (or four, or five or whatever their view might be about when it is 'possible' to diagnose). Again, we feel strongly that autism should be diagnosed as early as possible so that appropriate intervention can begin straight away. As one of the defining criteria of autism is that it should be evident in a child's development before they are three years old, it seems to us that most children should be diagnosed by this age and that, in many cases, it is possible to do so earlier.

Worrying about being wrong is one of the main reasons that some professionals give when they are reluctant to make an early diagnosis. They might be confident that the child has problems with, say, communication and some other aspects of development, but be uncertain whether or not he fits the 'whole pattern' of autism and want a bit longer to be sure enough to make a 'differential' diagnosis. In some cases this might be justified, although we would prefer to share with parents our thoughts that autism might be one of the possible explanations for the problems that their child is experiencing. An element of uncertainty about diagnosis shouldn't, though, delay appropriate support and intervention. The approach outlined in this book will be helpful to any child who has difficulties with language and communication.

WHAT ARE THE DEFINING CRITERIA FOR A DIAGNOSIS OF AUTISM?

Autism is diagnosed using what has come to be known as the 'triad of impairments': three main areas of difficulty that are apparent in a child's development before he is three years old. This doesn't mean that all children are diagnosed before they are three, but that through the careful taking of a history from the parents, together with other observations, it is clear that the pattern was starting to emerge before this age. These three areas of difficulty are:

- difficulty with language and communication

- difficulties in social relationships and social understanding
- a lack of flexibility in thinking and behaviour.

Autism is what is known as a 'pervasive development disorder', which means that each of these difficulties affects the others and it is easier to separate them on paper than it is in the child. It might be helpful, though, to briefly consider each area in turn, looking at the growing influence that autism has on a child's development.

Difficulty with language and communication

This affects the child's ability to make sense of, and use, all forms of language and communication. Crucially this affects not just spoken language but gesture, facial expression and other forms of body language. These 'building-blocks' to communication, which are known as pragmatics, are almost entirely biological in their origin and develop naturally in ordinary children. Babies spend most of their first year practising, and becoming more accomplished at, these skills so that when their first words appear they are able to slot them in to a 'framework of communication' that has already been established. It is the ability to do this that later enables children to use their speech for conversation. In children with autism these pragmatics are lacking, or severely disordered, and when their first words appear they are almost always used to 'label' the things they see or want and to repeat what they have heard other people say, often without meaning, rather than to enter into conversation with another person.

Difficulties in social relationships and social understanding

Young children with autism have often been described as 'aloof' or 'remote' and 'living in a world of their own'. While these are appropriate terms to describe some children, they are not for others. Many children, who seem quite socially active in certain situations and with familiar people, miss getting a diagnosis because of a misunderstanding of this. The social difficulty in autism is a lack of *social understanding* rather than of *social interest.* Some children may be interested in interaction with others, particularly in physical play like chasing games and rough and tumble, but do not know how to do it. One of the main objectives of this book, particularly the chapter on *Interactive Play,* is to give ideas about ways in which we can help the child do this more easily.

At the heart of this difficulty is a lack of *social empathy,* which means that he finds it very hard to understand what other people are thinking or feeling. Normally developing children have a 'hot line' to other people's thoughts and can, for example, read another person's facial expression to understand what they are thinking and predict what might happen. For example:

> Let's imagine an ordinary toddler, taken to visit somebody's house. On the mantlepiece he sees some glass ornaments that he thinks will be interesting to play with. Just as he reaches out for them he turns to look at his mum who frowns at him from across the room. He knows from this that she doesn't want him to touch them and will be able to have a fair guess at what she will say or do if he does! He can *understand* the unspoken message, *empathize* with what she is thinking and use this to *predict* what she will do.

One of the first signs of this ability to empathize with another person is when the toddler, who has just started to walk, brings things to people to show them, not because he wants them to do anything but just because he thinks they might be interested; and he wants to share that interest. The toddler with autism, if he brings things at all, is only likely to do this if he wants something done with it, such as a jar opened or a toy fixed.

Another of the most common, and early, features of this social difficulty is the nature of the child's eye-contact with other people. Sometimes this is enormously reduced in *quantity* (the amount of time that a child looks at you), more significantly it's striking in the way the *quality* is different (the way he uses this eye-contact). What the child with autism finds so hard is to share a look and a smile, for example when he is looking at a book with you, and looking away at the right time as well as glancing at your eyes. This brings us back to the pragmatics of language, of which using eye gaze is an important part.

A lack of flexibility in thinking and behaviour

This is shown in different ways according to the age, personality, interests and ability of the child. It can be seen when children develop repetitive movements, become fascinated by looking at particular patterns (often straight lines and circles), line up and arrange their toys rather than using them in an imaginative way, become very insistent on following certain routines such as the way they usually go to the shops, want to watch the same extract of video again and again or develop fascinations with particular types of toys or characters from stories or television.

These sorts of behaviours can be seen in young, normally developing children but in autism they last longer, are more intense in the interest that they hold for the child and can frequently become the reason for outbursts of panic and anger, when things don't happen in quite the way in which he had expected or wanted.

In part what seems to be happening is that because the child finds the world so confusing, as a result of his problems in understanding and communication, he clings to the things that do make sense because they are so familiar. The chapter on the *Beginnings of Structure* discusses in more detail some of the ways in which the child with autism may find the world confusing and ways in which we can help him start to make better sense of it.

3 TAKING THE FIRST STEPS

Our starting point in this book is that the building-blocks of communication in ordinary babies are almost entirely biological and developmental; they do not have to be taught as skills, but develop naturally and increase in complexity through practice during infancy. Babies use the pragmatics of language to create a structure for the speech that normally follows. In the case of young children with autism the core difficulty means that these building-blocks are not firmly in place. It follows that there is a need to focus on the development of pragmatics so that speech can develop in a more natural fashion and become more safely established. This book is aimed at helping parents develop a framework for communication with their child using an interactive approach. The central theme is that we should focus our efforts on improving a child's understanding of language, develop his own ability to communicate and help him to become more actively involved with other people and the world around him.

Each chapter is self-contained and can be read separately, which means that there is some overlap in the content. There is no definite order in which they should be read and the way in which you do this may be dependent on the stage of development your child has reached and what your own priorities are. Some individual chapters though, in our opinion, are best read after the content of other chapters has been explored. Where this is the case it is suggested in the introduction to each chapter.

- *Interactive Play* is based on the central theme of understanding the importance of developing the pragmatics of communication, and gives ideas on how you can join in and develop play between you to help your child become a more effective communicator.

- *The Beginnings of Structure* is intended to help our understanding of why it can be difficult for the child with autism to learn about people and the world around him. It goes on to give some ideas on how things might be improved for your child. It also talks about the danger of trying to tackle too much at once and how you might choose priorities and make a plan of action.

- *Teaching Pointing* has a much more specific focus on one of the key pragmatic skills, a gesture that typically developing children understand and use by the end of the first year of life. For children with autism it usually requires specific teaching but can then be a foundation for later communication with words.

- The chapter on *Understanding Language* recognizes that it is often easy to think a child understands more than he does because of the way he finds extra clues in what he sees. The chapter aims to increase your awareness so that you can help your child make more sense of what you say to him.

- *Moving Towards Spoken Language* builds on the development of those conversation skills that typically come before speech, looks at how gestures and using pictorial symbols can be a bridge to spoken language and gives ideas on how to encourage those first words and beyond.

- The last chapter, *Sharing Conceptual Play*, is rather different in content. It is the second chapter about play and extends some of the principles in *Interactive Play*, but is more about using play to encourage your child to develop his thinking, which is particularly important in children with autism where their difficulty in thinking flexibly often gets in their way of learning everyday concepts.

Parents have often asked us 'How much time should we spend on interactive play sessions or trying to structure his learning?' Of course there is no simple answer to this. It will depend on your circumstances, your child's personality and needs and what other forms of intervention he might be receiving at pre-school or from therapists, for example. Many of the ideas can be incorporated into everyday activities so that they make the most of naturally occurring exchanges between you. Structure and routine, though, can help both you and your child; daily interactive play sessions, or regular times that you set aside to encourage him to focus on toys and other activities, are definitely beneficial. The approach is about developing communication through shared enjoyment and fun, so above all enjoy yourselves!

4 INTERACTIVE PLAY

INTRODUCTION

This chapter is intended to help you find more ways of playing with your child that will encourage his communication skills. It includes ideas for playing and singing, based on several years of work by staff at Sutherland House School.

Before we can start to look at ways of helping your child become a better communicator, it may be useful to begin by thinking about communication and language, and how these *usually* develop.

In ordinary development, *spoken language* only begins once a child can already communicate many of his feelings, thoughts and intentions effectively by non-verbal means. Almost from birth, babies make a range of noises, facial expressions and actions, which adults naturally respond to as if the baby was actually speaking to them.

For example:

- A baby cries: his mum says 'I know, you're hungry, here you are...' as she gets ready to feed him.
- A baby squeals on her changing mat: her parent makes a similar high-pitched sound in response, and they have a little 'conversation' of vocal sounds.
- A baby gurgles and coos: a visiting adult turns to him immediately and says 'Hello! What is it? Are you telling me something? Really? Well I never!...' and so on.
- A baby screws up his face: his dad mirrors his expression as he says 'Oh dear! What is it?' 'Got a pain?' etc.

Over the first few months, because parents treat their baby's behaviour *as if* he had intended to communicate, he begins to try out *intentional communication*. Quickly there develops a *dialogue* between parent and child in which each takes distinct turns.

This dialogue consists of movements, exaggerated facial expressions, and various tuneful sounds, alongside the parent's spoken language and often involves humour and teasing. The baby and the adult both listen, watch, and (just as important) *pause* for each other's contributions, creating the two-way flow of conversation.

So ordinary babies spend their first year practising communication skills, and then have the relatively easy task of slotting words into this 'pattern of conversation' which is now *ready* for words. During this time babies are developing what is known as *communicative competence*.

For children with autism, early interaction is likely to be very different. These children have real difficulties in using and understanding all methods of communication, including facial expression, gesture, and all non-verbal skills as well as words. They also have difficulty with the development of *social timing*, which allows babies to interweave their communications with another person's, and develop the sort of dialogue that we've described.

The development of *shared attention* is vital in this process. Usually, babies are instinctively interested in the things that other people are doing or thinking. They watch them and copy them; they draw people's attention to things by pointing and bringing things to show them in a way that seems to say 'look at this...what do you think about it?' The child with autism has great difficulty with this and may prefer to do things on his own, finding it hard to realize the enjoyment in sharing.

All of this means that we need to help children with autism to *enter into and enjoy* interaction with other people, as a foundation for building further communication skills. Using interactive play as described in this chapter is an attempt to do just that.

FOLLOWING AND RESPONDING

Imitation

Much early learning about people takes place through imitation. However, in practice most babies learn to imitate adults *because their parents imitate them* to begin with. The baby sneezes, and his mother says 'Aa-tishoo! Got a cold, then?' and the baby smiles and may even pretend-sneeze again as part of the dialogue. By imitating their babies, parents help them appreciate the *significance* of their behaviour and, later, babies and children copy the things their parents do.

Deliberately copying a child's movements or vocal sounds can be a very productive and enjoyable way of achieving shared attention. In the early stages you might try:

- Imitating some of your child's vocal sounds as closely as you can. Try to match his pitch and volume as well as the rhythm and the actual sounds. If he doesn't seem to notice or doesn't stay focused for long, you could try vocalizing through a cardboard or plastic tube, or using a plastic 'echo mike' (or a real 'karaoke' type microphone), or other ways of exaggerating your responses.

- Letting him explore a drum or other simple sound-maker, and copying the actions and sounds he makes, even if they are not the conventional ones you would expect. You might get into a kind of *'conversation' without words*, where you can combine imitating him with adding an extra sound – see if he gives you eye-contact in surprise.

- Watching him play with a 'floaty' scarf or piece of material, then using a similar one yourself, 'mirroring' his posture and movements, and the shapes he is making.
- Joining in with him as he walks, jumps, stamps and stops. (You could combine this with a commentary as described below.)

Many children are fascinated by this reflecting of their own behaviour, and seem to become more aware of themselves and their own actions and sounds. Research has also shown that being copied by an adult increases the amount of time the child looks at that person's face. Once the child begins to produce a sound or action deliberately to have it copied, they are acting with *intentionality*.

Of course this kind of imitative play naturally occurs with very young babies, but children with autism may not respond in the same way. It may not seem so natural to play like this with a toddler or an older child. What we are trying to do is *re-introduce* this sort of play *in a very positive way* so that they appreciate the enjoyment that can be gained from shared experience and activities. They are also building up the skills of taking turns, using eye-contact and so on, which are vital to communication. *A starting point in encouraging the child to enter our social world is to join in with his.* Some children with autism seem to need us to do this a lot before they begin to be interested in copying *our* actions or sounds.

Commenting

Another way of trying to get across to your child that you are trying to 'tune in' to his world is to comment on what he is doing in his spontaneous play and behaviour. This commentary can be spoken, chanted or sung, and can vary in its complexity from single words to phrases and sentences.

Commenting is more likely to engage your child's attention and be meaningful to him if you keep the language simple and time it to coincide with his actions. You might do it to *show him that you know* what he's looking at, or wants ('Paul's looking at the tree', 'You want the book'), or to describe his play, or to accompany an everyday activity.

For example:

- James often spins round, and seems to be in his own world. His dad is watching him one day and he starts chanting quietly,

  Spinning, spinning

  James is spinning

  Round and round and round and round.

- When James stops, his father adds 'Stop!' This continues for a while, and he begins to look at his dad as he stops, anticipating the words. Over a few days they repeat this shared game, and eventually they can *both* start and stop the game, using eye-contact, movement and vocal sounds.

- Matthew is running up and down the hall, from the kitchen door to the front door, over and over again. His mum positions herself by the kitchen door, and crouches down to his level. As he carries on, she gently sings in time with his running:

  > Running to the door...and
  >
  > Running back to mummy!

  each time he does it.

- Matthew seems to notice: he hesitates at the front door and watches his mum as she extends the 'and...', building up the anticipation, before he runs back to her. A few days later, playing the same game, he suddenly runs to the stairs and enjoys hearing the new version, 'Running to the stairs!'

- When Sarah is in the bath, she likes splashing but not being washed. Her dad sings as he tries to wash her: 'Washing Sarah's feet' (to the tune of 'Knees up Mother Brown') and she tolerates being washed. He sings a 'splashing' verse in between when she splashes. Over a few weeks, she starts to cooperate and even help with washing, enjoys choosing which part of her body will be washed next, and makes encouraging noises to get her dad to sing the commentary.

- Thomas is pushing his train round the track, silently, watching the wheels. His dad comes and joins him on the floor and watches. He starts commenting, saying ‘Pushing the train…round the bend… Over the bridge!’ in time with Thomas’s actions. The commentary takes on a rhythmic, chanting sound. Thomas is still focused on the train but occasionally starts to look up at his dad, sometimes pausing in his game. After a while, if his dad stops commenting Thomas looks up and makes a 'p' sound. Dad answers 'Push! Yes, push! Pushing the train…' and the game continues. Gradually the game is extended as his dad comments on any small variation Thomas makes, or adds the occasional idea himself.

- When Joey is looking out of the window, his mum comes and stands beside him and starts to sing 'We're looking out of the window, looking out of the window, looking out of the window, to see what we can see…' (to the tune of 'For He's a Jolly Good Fellow'). She follows Joey's gaze: he is looking at a car. She carries on with the song 'We can see a *car*, we can see a *car*, car on the road…' etc. and she points to the car. Joey keeps looking at the car, but if his mum pauses in the song, he looks at her to continue. Over the next few weeks, this game develops on the bus as well as at home and nursery. Joey looks at lots of different things and even begins to *point* to draw his mum's attention to things to sing about. (See the chapter on *Teaching Pointing* for the importance of this gesture.)

One of the main benefits of this type of commentary is that your child will hear language that is *meaningful* and *relevant* to him at the time. It also shows him that you are aware of and interested in the things that he is doing. Also it may be that, in the same way that he produces actions and sounds with the intention of getting you to copy them, he may do this to get you to *comment* on them. This intentionality is crucial in his developing communication.

CREATING A FRAMEWORK FOR COMMUNICATION

Sometimes, following and responding to your child as we've described leads to a situation where you can really get into a two-way 'conversation', even if it is at a very basic level. At other times, it helps if you bring in short repetitive play routines and familiar songs, which can act as a 'framework' for conversation.

Play routines

Play routines are those short repetitive games that adults tend to play instinctively with young children and babies. Some are well known, and passed down the generations, like 'peek-a-boo'. Others are made up just through playing with your own child and repeating what he enjoys. These games often involve physical contact or 'rough and tumble' play, and many parents of children with autism find that they can feel closer to their child at these times than in calmer or softer exchanges – though this will come.

Play routines of this type may be non-verbal, but usually contain simple, repetitive language, and include an element of anticipation before the climax.

Examples are:

I'm coming to…swing you round!	(where you do an action to your child)
1 2 3…tickle!	"
And…tickle you under there!	"
Charlie goes…Crash!	(which may be built up by copying what your child likes doing)
And…jump!	"
Here we go…spin!	"

Careful use of *timing, pacing* and *pausing* in these games makes the difference between simply having a good time, and giving opportunities to develop communication skills in an enjoyable, shared play situation.

For example, once you have found a play routine that you both enjoy, you can try:

- Building up the tension (by getting slower and louder), and then *pausing* silently just *before* the key point, for your child to anticipate.

- Responding to small signs of anticipation at this point (e.g. a look, a movement or a sound) by continuing immediately.

- Repeating the game and pausing to help your child indicate *intentionally* that he wants the game to continue.

Later on, you might extend and vary your play routines, to help him enjoy more flexibility, and make meaningful choices. For example, he might choose between a swing and a tickle, by using gestures, movements, sounds or words.

Action songs

Singing with your child can be a relaxed and enjoyable way of getting his attention and sharing an activity. You don't need a wonderful singing voice to do the things suggested here – just enthusiasm and a willingness to 'tune in' to your child's choices and responses.

Set songs

Set action songs, such as 'Wind the Bobbin' or 'Row Your Boat', are often very popular with young children. They enjoy the repetition, and may begin to watch, anticipate or join in with some of the actions. Once you have found a song that your child likes, you can vary the speed and timing to give him opportunities to take part, in the same way as in play routines.

For example, you might:

- Try *pausing dramatically* sometimes before a favourite action within a song. Eventually the child may slot in an action, sound or word on purpose when you pause, but to start with you may have to respond *as if* he did. (If you use a certain song a lot, it's best not to pause *every* time at the same point, otherwise the pause becomes part of the routine and loses its impact.)

- Slow down a familiar song, so that he is able to get 'one step ahead' of you at certain points and *lead you* by making eye-contact, body movements, sounds or words.

- Contrast fast and slow or loud and soft when you repeat a song, so that he can show a preference and eventually *make a choice.*

Flexible songs

Flexible action songs such as 'This is the Way We Stamp Our Feet' (to the tune of 'Here We Go Round the Mulberry Bush'), and so on are very useful for creating a framework for communication. Unlike the set songs, the words are not exactly the same each time you sing them, and you can respond to your child's mood and preferences moment by moment.

In the early stages, you can use these songs for:

- Singing about what *you* are doing with your child, e.g. 'This is the way we swing you round', etc.

- Singing about what your child is doing of his own accord – e.g. 'This is the way we walk around', and so on. This links with the earlier section on 'Following and responding'. Like giving a commentary, making a verse about what your child is doing may help you to get his attention and enable him to do more actions on purpose.

- Offering ideas for your child to watch or copy, such as 'This is the way we rub our hands', etc. But don't forget that it's usually *easier for him to produce actions for you* to copy, rather than imitating you. Even so, once you have copied some of his actions, he may start to show interest in trying to copy yours. It can be a good interactional game, either way round.

- Giving him a clear opportunity to *choose* an action: as soon as you have found two actions he enjoys, you can pause at 'This is the way we…?'

Some other tunes that can be used flexibly, in a similar way to the 'Mulberry Bush' example, are:

Drunken sailor	e.g. What shall we do with Thomas Mason…? We'll pat, pat, pat his knees…etc.
Skip to my Lou	e.g. Clap, clap, clap your hands…etc.

DEVELOPING 'GIVE AND TAKE'

Some of the ideas we have suggested may start to go well for you and your child, and you are building up a range of games and songs that you both enjoy. So where do you go from here?

In the early stages, you may find that the interaction is rather one-sided. Some children are only interested if everything is on their terms and you follow their lead; others can only be 'engaged' if you keep providing familiar games and songs. This is fine at first, but gradually you can move towards more of a 'balance', like a good conversation. The eventual aim is to *share the control in a flexible way.* This may take a very long time to achieve for some children.

As you start to move towards a more equal balance of control with your child, you might try some of the following:

- Look out for moments in your shared play where you can *tease* each other in a gentle way – maybe by doing something unexpected in a familiar game, or pausing longer than usual, creating an *element of surprise.*
- If he enjoys *leading* an imitation game, you can start slipping in some sounds or movements you know he likes, to see if he will follow you. If he does, you can gradually introduce slight variations and different actions or sounds. At any point, though, you might need to go back to following him, so as not to lose the flow.

- If he is very keen on set routines and songs, you might try to extend them to be more flexible, take turns to choose one, or try to create a 'space' between them for something more spontaneous to happen.
- *Within* flexible action songs, you can adjust the balance of who leads and who follows, from verse to verse.

FINALLY

Interactive play can be a really enjoyable and effective way to help your child practice some of the most vital skills needed for communication. The ideas in this chapter are aimed at getting him *actively* involved in interaction so that he gets used to sharing interests, looking, listening and taking turns. This kind of play is called *reciprocal play*, and it gives the child a taste of the *social empathy* that is so difficult for children with autism. But once he is doing these things, he will be able to learn much more in all kinds of ways from the people around him.

You may already have developed some games and songs to build on in the ways suggested here, or you might feel you have to start from scratch. If your child is not responsive at first, do persist in your attempts to play. This does *not* mean forcing him into things he really doesn't like, but sometimes it does take a few repetitions before a child realizes that what you are offering might be fun. It's hard to keep going when you feel you are getting little or no positive response, but bear in mind how difficult it might be for him to make sense of your face, gestures and words.

You will also need to adapt these activities, and your approach, to suit your own and your child's personalities, and his particular needs and preferences. For example, some people find their child is most easily engaged by a dramatic, 'over-the-top' style, with exaggerated facial expressions and tone of voice. For other children this is totally overwhelming and off-putting, and you may even need to 'tone down' your voice, face and actions to encourage your child to watch and take part in the games and songs.

Above all, this approach is about helping communication through *mutual enjoyment.* Play is not play if it is forced. We hope you will take and adapt some of these ideas to help your child develop the basic framework for communication. Once he is using these basic skills, he is more likely to develop sounds, gestures and words, and to use them intentionally, in a context which is meaningful for him and for you.

5 THE BEGINNINGS OF STRUCTURE

INTRODUCTION

This chapter is intended to help our understanding of how children learn about people and the world around them; and it will look at some of the ways in which this is difficult for the child with autism. It will also give some ideas of how things could be improved for your child.

First of all it might be helpful to try to picture what the world is like for *any* baby. To start with it must be a very confusing place with lots of sounds and movements rushing past at random. Gradually, though, the baby starts to learn that the world has some organization and order; that is, it has *structure*. Over the first few weeks she starts to be able to follow movements with her eyes, guess where sounds are coming from and think about what they mean. She soon begins to be able to predict what will happen at certain times, or during certain activities. She learns that some of the things that she does have particular effects; and that the noises and babble that she makes have outcomes in what other people do or say back to her. The baby's interest in *people* gives her the key to learning how the world works. In this way the world starts to *make sense* to her.

For a child with autism this is not nearly so straightforward, and the world can continue to be a confusing, unpredictable and, at times, frightening place. People's voices and body language have little meaning to him. As a result he might become withdrawn and 'switched off' from people, often becoming more and more absorbed in very repetitive activities that help him feel secure. He may begin to show his confusion by behaving in a rather 'panicky' way. In this chapter, and the others in the series, we think about ways of helping your child develop his understanding of the world and other people as early as possible. In this way we hope to reduce both his sense of isolation and his outbursts of anxious, panicky or angry behaviour.

WHY IS IT DIFFICULT FOR A CHILD WITH AUTISM TO MAKE SENSE OF HIS WORLD?

Every child with autism has his *own distinct personality*, in the same way as any other child. In addition to this, the *severity of autism* will vary from one child to the next, and so will *other learning difficulties* that he may have. Therefore some children will find 'making sense' harder than others. Some of the most common difficulties found among children with autism are in these early childhood abilities:

- *attending* to other people
- understanding the *language and intentions of others*
- *communicating* their needs and wishes to other people
- *cooperating* with people and understanding their expectations
- *enjoying people's company* and wanting to join in
- being able to *learn from experimental play* and not getting too fascinated by just one or two activities
- *playing with ideas* – for instance, *pretending*
- being *flexible in their response* to everyday activities
- interpreting some of their *sensory experiences*
- understanding everyday *sequences* of events and using these to *predict what might happen.*

HOW CAN WE HELP THE CHILD WITH AUTISM START TO MAKE BETTER SENSE OF THE WORLD?

Helping the development of any child with special needs involves two important elements.

- The first of these is to assess, as carefully as we can, the particular *areas that he is weak in* and use this information to plan a very individual programme aimed at *remedying* some of these weaknesses. For a child with autism it is likely that these weak areas will include communication and interaction with other people. Improving these will be a priority and we will need to choose some specific objectives to help him reach the next stage of development.

- The other element is to think about your child's *strengths and interests* so that you can build on these and use them to organize both the environment and the people around him in a way that *compensates* for some of his problems. For example, it might be that he is very good at identifying, and knowing the difference between, pictures and shapes. We could use this ability to explain what we are doing by showing him pictures to let him know what the next activity will be. For the moment this will help to overcome the difficulties he has when we use only words as an explanation. There will be more about using pictures and photographs later.

In the two sections that follow, we will suggest practical ways of helping a child with autism by introducing more *structure* (and therefore *meaning*) to help his understanding. The first section discusses how we can *plan out* what will be most helpful for this particular

child; the second looks at what we can *actually do* to make things easier for him in different areas of daily living.

So this chapter emphasizes how structure can help both you and your child, while *Understanding Language* emphasizes language itself; but inevitably they overlap.

SECTION 1: PLANNING AN INDIVIDUAL PROGRAMME

It is very important to *plan* what we want to achieve and how we are going to go about it. This starts with understanding precisely what our child can and can't do. Then we can work out priorities for the things that we want to encourage and change, and set objectives that are small enough for both our child and us to achieve. It helps if we reach agreement with everyone concerned about the methods we are going to use.

Without a plan we can find ourselves trying to do a bit of everything and never seeing anything through. This means that the child does not experience success, and neither do we.

Working out what our child can and can't do

The first step here is to build up a *full* picture of our child's abilities across all of the areas of development: his movement, his language and other ways of communicating, his thinking and his social behaviour. If your child has already had some form of developmental assessment, at a child development centre for example, then this is something that the professional workers will have tried to establish. If you haven't yet had this kind of assessment, it might be helpful for you to try this yourself. A list of different areas of development that might be looked at in an assessment could include the following headings:

- general social behaviour and mood
- imitation
- following instructions
- reciprocal play (sharing, turn-taking and interaction)
- hand–eye coordination
- whole body movement
- expressive language (what your child says)

- receptive language (what your child understands)
- non-verbal communication (the 'pragmatics')
- cognitive (problem-solving) skills
- pretend play (sometimes called symbolic or imaginative play).

Sometimes we can see very clearly what a child can and can't do, but in some situations it may be much more difficult. The chapter on *Understanding Language* gives some examples of this. For instance, if your child moves towards the front door when you say 'We're going out to the shops', is that because he understood what you were saying – or is it because he saw that you had your coat on and had the keys in your hand?

Sometimes we may need to 'test out' our observations more carefully to ensure that we know what they mean. For instance, we might try saying 'We're going out to the shops' *before* putting a coat on, and at a time he isn't expecting this, so that he's not guessing from the situation. This doesn't mean that we're trying to 'catch him out'; we just need to be as accurate as we can. It's good that he uses the situation to guess, but *we need to know* if he understands the words too. We are not helping our child if we overestimate what he can do or how much he understands because we would then, probably, make things too complicated for him.

Of course, when children are very young they often change quite quickly, so this information needs to be updated regularly. Doing this may also allow us to be aware of the progress he is making and to see how effective our efforts have been.

Choosing priorities and setting objectives

There may be many things that we would like our child to learn that he isn't doing at the moment, such as communicating more or showing more interest in a range of toys. There are also probably a number of things he does that we would rather he did *less* of – hitting out when he gets cross, for instance, or wanting to watch the same DVD over and over again. We can't try to tackle all of these things at once, and so we have to make decisions about *what our priorities should be.*

Priorities will be very individual to both your own child and your particular circumstances. You might choose something as a priority because it is something he is *almost* doing now but with a little bit of help could do rather better. For example, maybe he's taking you to something he wants and pushing your hand in the right direction, but not yet pointing to it himself. Or you might choose something that, once he has learned it, will help him to do lots of other things. An example of this is learning to attend to his own name so that he will then be more likely to listen to the things that you say to him.

You might feel that *reducing* something he does now is important because it's getting in the way of other things. Maybe he always insists on holding a particular toy, or other object, which then prevents him from exploring other things.

It is also worth considering yourself and your needs when choosing the most important priorities to work on. For example, if your child is awake a lot in the night, this is likely to make you more tired and irritable, and might mean that you're not able to spend as much time playing with him and working to improve his communication.

This book is about using '*frameworks for communication*' in an *interactive* way to help young children with autism. The central theme is that we should focus our efforts on improving a child's *understanding of language* (receptive language), develop his own *ability to communicate* (expressive language) and help him to become more actively *involved with other people* (reciprocal play). This means that when choosing new skills to develop, we will want to include all of these areas, and that we will also include non-verbal language (such as eye-contact and pointing) alongside spoken language.

Agreeing on methods to use

Some of the methods that we can use to encourage communication and learning, or to avoid or deal with difficult behaviour, are discussed here and some are taken further in other chapters.

You need to discuss and agree with any other people involved just how you are going to go about this. Talk to other people in the family and any professional workers such as playgroup or nursery staff, speech and language therapists, and so on. It is important that everyone knows what the others are doing, so that different people have the same expectations of your child and deal with his behaviour as consistently as possible. It can be a good idea to keep a diary of what you decide, so that you remember the details of what you're trying to do and why, share the ideas with other people, and make notes about what actually happens.

The example below comes from John's individual programme. It sets out objectives in one particular area of development (receptive language), and gives a description of how these can be worked on.

Receptive language (what John understands)

	Objectives	*Action*
1.	John to become more responsive to his name, and to be able to attend to others' language (speech and simple gestures).	Use 'John…' at the *beginning* of sentences when talking to John to make it clear that I'm talking to *him* (and maybe tap his shoulder or touch his face to check this and remind him to look). Try making up hiding games where I call out his name so that he can find me (such as hide under sheets or duvet, or behind furniture).

2. To develop his 'situational' understanding and move towards *associating words* with certain situations and activities.	Give John lots of visual clues to situations (like showing him his coat or a photograph of it when it's time to go out), together with simple and appropriate language. Sometimes I might try giving him a verbal prompt *without* any situational or visual clues to see whether he is able to respond yet.
3. To associate *simple gestures* with situations (e.g. gestures that mean come here, sit down, give me).	Use a range of simple gestures *alongside* speech. Decide on consistent gestures for the same meaning (e.g. beckoning for 'come here', open hand for 'give me') so that we all use the same.
4. To develop his understanding of simple words, including nouns (shoes, coat, body parts, etc.), action words (such as bouncing, tickle) and other words (such as up, down).	Use *simple* repetitive language as a commentary to what he is doing (e.g. '*Shoes* on', 'Going up…and *down*'), and emphasize the 'key' words within sentences. When John is absorbed with looking at pictures or photographs, continue to name the objects that he is looking at (or pointing to). Try to keep it playful, maybe by varying intonation or saying the word and the associated sound – miaow! Or trying to take a turn where *I* point and wait for John to name. Carry on asking him to show me things (e.g. asking 'Where's the…?'). I'll try to keep a list of words that he definitely understands.

SECTION 2: ORGANIZING OURSELVES AND THE ENVIRONMENT

One of the most important ways of helping your child make better sense of the world is to think carefully about how to improve his understanding of the messages and information that he receives. If he finds it hard to learn about how the world works, then we need to try to create much more *structure* to help him. We can do this in three main ways:

- *clarifying the language* that we use to him
- *organizing his day* to make it more predictable
- *structuring* some of his play and learning.

Clarifying the language we use

Earlier we talked about how important it is to have as clear an idea as possible about what your child can and can't do. We saw that knowing how much language he understands is not always straightforward. People living and working with children who have autism do often overestimate how much language they understand, and try to get things across to the child in a way that is too complicated. If you are to help your child understand as much as possible, you really need to adjust your language to his ability. Here are some points that you might find helpful.

- *Make sure you have his attention when you speak to him.* Often when we start to speak to a child with autism he doesn't attend to us, and in fact many parents at first wonder about their child's hearing. It might be that he is busy with something else, or that he simply hasn't noticed us, or he hasn't seen the signs that we're talking to *him* and not to someone else. Listening to someone usually involves *shifting attention* from one thing to another; but children with autism often find this difficult.

Get in the habit of always using his name at the start rather than the end of a sentence: 'James – get your coat on' rather than 'Get your coat on, James'. Remember that he may not even be aware of you until you say his name, so saying it at the end can mean he misses the message entirely! You might need to cut down on *distractions* by turning the television off or getting him to put down the toy he's fiddling with. It might be useful to touch him lightly, or take hold of his hand when you start speaking to him or

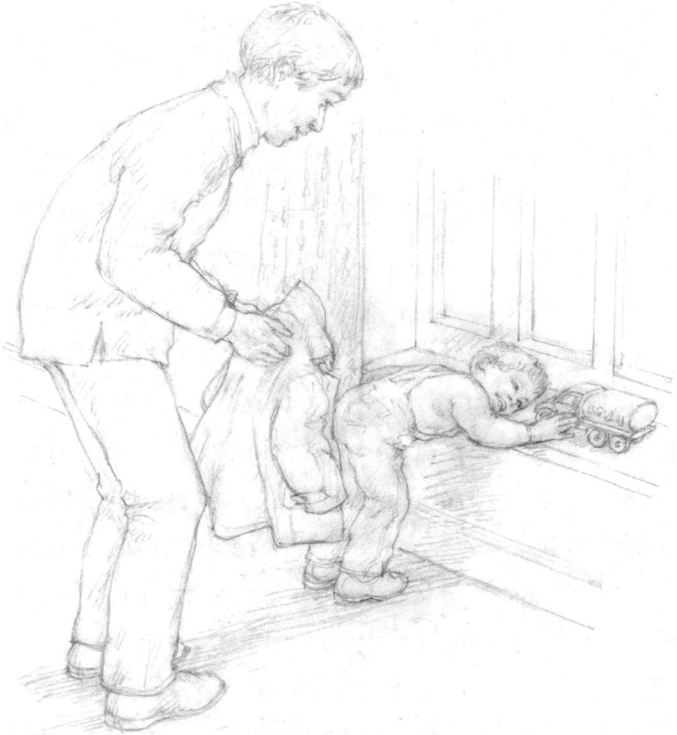

blow gently on his cheek. All of these things can act as signals to him that you are *about* to say something to him: so that he gets ready to listen *before* the message, not after it.

- *Use shorter phrases and emphasize key words.* When we talk in everyday language, a lot of what we say is unnecessary information; that is, we don't need to understand it in order to follow what is being said. Ordinary children very quickly learn to pick out what's important and make sense of it. Children with autism find this much harder and need more help. Which of the following examples would be easier for your child to understand?

  Okay then, James, why don't we turn off the television for a moment? Then we can go into the kitchen and get ourselves a drink and something to eat.

  James...television off...*it's time for a* drink *and a* cake.

- *Add visual clues to what you say.* Children with autism find it easier to understand information that they can see because this doesn't require them to understand language. For example, your child may well be able to understand that it's teatime when he sees you set a plate and his cup at the kitchen table, but not when you call out 'it's teatime' to him when he's in another room. When we set out deliberately to use visual information to make messages clearer, this is known as *visual clarification.* There are several different types of visual clues that we can use according to different situations and how much help a child needs.

  For instance, we can show him an *object* as we tell him what's happening. In the above example this might mean showing him the plate as we tell him 'it's teatime'. Some parents find it helpful to keep a collection of objects that can be used in this way at different points in the day. These are sometimes referred to as '*objects of reference*' and they can help to provide a link between the word and the activity or event it *refers* to.

We can use *photographs, pictures* or *symbols* (line drawings of an object or event) in the same way as objects; if your child is able to understand them, they are more convenient to use. Sometimes it is enough to show him the picture before the activity; sometimes the child might carry the picture with him. For some children, when they are first learning the pictures or symbols, it can be useful to have pairs that match. For example, you might show your child a photo or symbol of a bath when you are downstairs, which he then carries with him and 'matches' with the identical picture that you have stuck to the bathroom door. As well as using pictures one at a time before familiar activities, such as bath-time or going to the car, two or more might also be used to explain a *sequence* of events: for example, 'first *dinner* then *television*' or 'first *shop* then *swings*'.

These examples include symbols from the Makaton[1] vocabulary. Some children also find pictures or photographs helpful that you have taken of the supermarket, the local park, and so on. There is no golden rule; use whatever is easier for your child and yourself. A lot of children really benefit from these sequences of pictures. They can be built on to become 'timetables', which we will discuss in a moment.

first  then 

dinner television

first  then 

shop swings

- *Use a clear consistent gesture alongside a key word.* You might make a beckoning gesture when you say 'come here', or mime drinking as you say 'do you want a *drink*?' Although children with autism don't find it *easy* to pick up on these cues from our natural gesture and body language (which is why they have difficulty with pointing), they *are* often helped if you use a small range of gestures, purposefully and clearly.
- The same is true of *hand signs* (such as those from the Makaton vocabulary) which are an extension of natural gesture. When adults use signs they are giving the child visual information, *alongside* the spoken word. They are also likely to be speaking more slowly, emphasizing key words and using short consistent phrases. Signs can also *last longer*, which gives the child more time to take in the information.

It is important that for the moment we are talking about using signs to help your child *understand*. We are not suggesting that you should expect him to sign back to you. The communication of *some* children with autism is eventually helped by their using signs and, for many, it does actually help their speech. Using signs himself, though, tends to come later in a child's development. It should only be encouraged when we are sure that he can do a number of other things: understanding the *names* of a lot of objects, understanding a *range of gestures*, being able to *imitate our* actions and being able to *point for the things he wants.*

- *Avoiding use of open-ended questions at this stage.* An open-ended question is one that has many possible answers; for instance 'What do you want to play with?' A closed question is where you restrict the possibilities, for example 'Do you want the bike or the swing?'

  Children with autism find making choices very difficult and in speech they are often helped by a closed question because this already suggests the possible answers.

- *Demonstrate what you mean alongside what you say.* There may be times when, however clear you make what you say, your child still doesn't respond. This may be because, in spite of your efforts, he still hasn't understood. Alternatively, it might be that he'd rather be getting on with something else instead. Sometimes it is helpful to physically guide him through the action you want of him: for example, gently guiding him to the chair as you say 'sit down' and then carrying on *as if* he'd done it himself. We'll return to this idea in the section on structuring play and learning.

Organizing your child's day

It is a feature of autism that children have a strong sense of order and routine. While we need to be careful that this doesn't develop into a rigidity that rules the lives of the family, we can use it to help make the world more predictable (and therefore reassuring) for the child. One of the reasons that children with autism can have outbursts of agitation or distress is that they find it hard to predict what is going to happen, particularly when there are changes to their usual routine. It is also difficult for them to understand when you try to explain what they are going to do next, or why they can't do what they had expected, or what they might be doing, instead.

For any young child, but more so for children with autism, a familiar routine does help them feel secure, and reduces anxiety. When something becomes part of their routine, they can accept and enjoy it more.

Structure and routine can help us too. You'll be less likely to miss out on your child's interactive play session if you get into the habit of making it a regular half-hour before lunch every day. In the same way, if you make a time to play with toys after breakfast each morning, *before* he starts watching his videos, you can then get on doing something else for a while without feeling you should be doing something with him! *Allocating time* in this way also means that you can balance the things that you want to do and give more time to whatever you have chosen as priorities.

When children start at a fairly structured nursery or school, you often see quite a change in their behaviour because they like the order and routine of the day. They can predict that when the teacher starts to clear away the activities, it's going to be time for them to sit on the rug for a story; they know that when singing finishes they will be expected to carry their chair to the table for a drink. As well as becoming familiar with these *daily routines*, they also start to build up some understanding of a *weekly structure* – that there are school days and home days, and that, for example, swimming happens once a week on a particular day. Of course, school and home are different places and you probably wouldn't choose to lead your life in such an ordered fashion. At the same time, some structure and a simple timetable will probably help you to help your child.

The last section introduced the idea of using pictures or symbols to 'back up' our verbal explanations. Many children find a '*visual timetable*' helpful. If your child has begun to understand that symbols or photographs represent familiar events, you can begin to use them to show him the idea of '*first this, then that*', as in the examples given earlier. As your child understands this process better and his vocabulary of symbols builds up, the timetable can be extended. For example, you might be able to use three or four (or more) together to show him that 'first it's *play with toys*, then watch the *television*, then *bath*, then *bed*'. If you do get to this stage, it is going to be important to decide how you present the symbols. Some children like them kept in order in a photograph wallet that they can take about with them, but sometimes backing the pictures with Velcro® so that they can be fixed to a felt-covered board can be helpful. You might like to put this on the wall of the kitchen and show it to your child regularly. Later on he'll probably come to look at it for himself, to check what's going to happen.

If your child does find it hard to accept or tolerate changes to his usual routine, this sort of system can be very helpful in explaining a change. For example, you might usually visit his granny's on the way home from swimming but today (perhaps because she's on holiday) you're going to the park instead. Showing your child this

on a timetable won't always placate him, but he *is* more likely to understand; and many children with autism are, in fact, much more accepting of change if they can see it in this visual way.

STRUCTURING PLAY AND LEARNING

Other chapters in this book look at early social play (*Interactive Play*) and play that helps your child explore ideas (*Sharing Conceptual Play*). As well as this, though, there are times when we need to give some thought to how we can build a bit more structure into a child's play and learning experiences. The principles are the same as those in the rest of this chapter. We want to make things as clear to the child as we possibly can. We want to help him see the *purpose and possibilities* of a particular toy or activity, and show him how to succeed.

One of the first problems you might encounter is simply *attracting your child's interest* in the toy or activity that you have selected. Use what you have already learned by choosing a short period each day when you can spend time playing with him. This would apply equally to interactive play and play with toys (which can be interactive in a different way). Choose a time when you know that you don't have to attend to other things, and when he can learn to predict that a play session is going to happen: for instance after breakfast or when he's had his bath. Make sure, as far as you can, that there aren't going to be other things to distract him or you, and explain 'It's time to play with *toys*'.

For this it might be helpful to start off with a favourite toy that you only use for these sessions and show it to him before you start; later on you might want to show a symbol or picture as we have described. Using this, you can then bring him to the place where you are going to carry out the session.

Sitting at a small table is really helpful for many young children with autism. It seems to help them get organized; and presenting each toy separately on the table will enable your child to focus his attention on that toy. 'Sitting up' on a chair tends to increase muscle tone, which can also improve his mental focus. If a small table isn't available, or he resists sitting on a chair, you could try putting the toys, again one at a time, on a small plain-coloured rug or a large tray. The message you are trying to get across is that this toy is the most interesting thing to look at, and that this space is where he concentrates on this kind of play. Again, you are using his love of routine to help him.

Think about your position in relation to his. It will be *easier for him to give you eye-contact* if you are opposite or at right angles to him; and try not to tower over him! You might prefer to kneel if the table is small.

As we've said, it's best to choose the toys that you use for this sort of session quite carefully, and it is likely to motivate him more if they are kept especially for these sessions. To start with, choose toys that you think he's most likely to be interested in; perhaps he likes toys that can spin or ones that make satisfying sounds (the chapter on *Conceptual Play* will give you lots of ideas). Later on you will start to choose toys that help him learn particular things that are important to his development.

It usually helps if the toys that you are going to use later in the session are at first kept out of sight, *so that he isn't distracted* from what you want him to attend to now. Keeping these in a separate box at the side of the table is often helpful. Sometimes it is useful to use a second box for the toys that are 'finished'. As he gets used to play sessions, this enables him to see the toys that you are going to show him during the session, and those that you've finished with, so that he knows what's left for him to do.

Don't expect to do very many activities in the early sessions; too many can make him bored or discouraged. If this happens he will learn to think of play as a struggle, and you probably will too! Start with two or three activities and build up at a pace that is right for your child. Try to finish each session on a positive note.

Too many activities may be discouraging, but so is doing *too much* at once or going on *too long*. It's best to start with small steps and build up from there. For example, he might find it quite hard to put shapes into an inset puzzle, so when you tip all the pieces out he soon gets frustrated. It's much better to take out just one or two pieces that he can replace and then he can see that he's finished, and end on success.

Even though we have called this *structured* play and learning, do remember that it's meant to be fun for both of you. This may not seem to be the case at first, and you may find your child resists and becomes unhappy or angry. This might be because he's confused and doesn't yet know what to expect. Following the principles of *familiar routines* and *clarity of communication* should help with this.

Alternatively, any reluctance may be because he doesn't attend for long enough to see the 'pay-off' or climax in a particular toy; or perhaps he hasn't built up a sense of success, and doesn't even know when he has been successful. You need to make the session as rewarding as possible for *him*. This starts with choosing the activities that you think *he* will be most interested in; but this still may not be enough.

You might need to find other ways of rewarding him until he learns to find that the reward is in the activity itself. For now he might need lots of praise, or blowing bubbles or winding a musical toy at the end of each activity. Different children find different things rewarding, and you may need to use some ingenuity; you'll find other ideas in the *Sharing Conceptual Play* chapter. Remember you are not trying to bribe your child into being cooperative, but to make it very clear to him, so that he can understand that he has been successful.

What if you have chosen toys that are most likely to interest him, carefully explained and shown what's expected, broken the activity down into small steps and tried lots of rewards, but he *still* protests or refuses to cooperate? Persist a bit longer. It may be that he still hasn't stayed with something long enough to find out that it can be fun for him. You may need to demonstrate how to complete the activity. This might mean that you gently put your hand over his, pick up the inset shape together, place it in the board and reward him *as if* he'd done it himself. This is the same principle, *giving him the experience of success*, which we talk about in the *Teaching Pointing* chapter.

If this is still unsuccessful, it could be that he isn't really ready for this degree of structure and these sorts of demands. If this is the case you might do better, for the moment, spending more time on less structured interactive play; or maybe introducing toys to him in a less directive way. For example, you might leave the inset puzzle with one or two pieces balanced on the edge of their holes, and see whether he will complete what you have started, in his own time, perhaps when your back is turned! You can then return to using a more structured approach at a later date.

NOTE

1. Makaton is a language programme that uses signs, symbols and speech to enable people with learning and communication disabilities to communicate.

   The Makaton symbols shown on page 60 are covered by copyright and are included with permission from The Makaton Charity (www.makaton.org). More information can be gained from The Makaton Charity.

6 TEACHING POINTING

INTRODUCTION
Why teach pointing?

Children with autism have difficulty with *all* methods of communicating: not only with speech, but also with the 'body languages' of gesture and facial expression, as well as with more subtle kinds of body language. Ordinary children (and adults) use body language all the time, alongside their speech, both to understand other people and to make themselves understood. Ordinary babies communicate with body language right through the first year of life; what's more, they do it *intentionally*. Children with autism don't know how to do this properly.

Pointing is the first and most important gesture. A gesture is a signal that someone makes *intending it to be seen and understood by someone else.* Usually the person making the gesture tries to make eye-contact with the person it's intended for, to make sure they've received the message.

Lots of children with autism will *reach with their whole hand* for something they want off a high shelf, and maybe cry when they can't get it, but don't give their parents eye-contact – they just go on looking at the thing they want. Parents often treat this *as if* it were a gesture, and come to help the child, and this is a natural thing to do. However, reaching is not really a gesture because the child did not intend it as a signal – for him it was simply an action that failed to produce results.

In a similar way, some children take their father's or mother's hand and put it on what they want help with – a tap, a door-handle or a push-button perhaps – or even *throw* the hand at the shelf they want to reach. Again, this is not really a message to you as a person; they don't look at you to check whether you understood. What they are doing is sometimes described as 'using your hand as a tool', rather than seeking help from you as an individual.

- The most important reason for teaching pointing is that we want our child to realize that communication – making signals to people – is really useful to him and might also bring him pleasure. Most young children with autism don't realize this. We want them to gesture intentionally.

But why not just teach words?

Of course, all parents of children with autism long to hear their children talk to them. But in normal language development, babies follow a pointing gesture, and point themselves, before they develop words. There are usually logical reasons why certain things develop in a particular order; and when children need special help to develop, that help will usually be more effective if it follows the natural order, unless there are particular reasons for changing it. When we come to teach words, a child with autism will do better if we have helped him to understand *and use* body language first.

Ordinary babies don't need to be taught body language; children with autism do need that teaching. By teaching the simple forms of body language first, we will give them the underlying structure they need in order to get ready for spoken language.

When we take an ordinary nine-month-old out in her buggy, point to a duck and say 'Look! A duck!', she follows our pointing finger and is rewarded by seeing the duck. But, more important, she experiences *understanding our abstract signal* – because the pointing finger doesn't actually look like a duck, nor does the word particularly sound like a duck. Soon she is pointing to things herself

– usually before her first birthday – and expects us to look even if she has no words. This gives her enormous *power to communicate – to grab our attention.* Once she realizes this, her interest in communicating takes a great leap forward, and she experiments with other ways of using gesture and sounds intentionally, much more effectively than just crying.

- So the second major reason for teaching pointing is to give our child the *easiest* signal that will give him quick results.

Why not teach him a sign for something he likes, such as 'cake'?

Well, we might do that later on, but for the moment we just want to teach him one gesture, so as not to confuse him. This is all new to him, so we concentrate on one thing at a time. Besides, we are trying to make pointing *meaningful to him*, as we shall see in a moment. How many times in a day will we be prepared to give him a cake when he makes a 'cake' sign? We want to give him a gesture that is all-purpose, so that we can respond meaningfully whenever he points – 50 or a 100 times a day if necessary. This way he will get plenty of practice.

- So a third important reason for teaching pointing is to give him a *versatile* gesture – one that he can use in many different situations. Not only that, but a versatile gesture means he can point for what *he* wants – not just for the things we have given him signs or words for.

There is another rather similar reason, which is about the stage our child has reached in understanding what language is *for*.

No child is born knowing what the rest of us easily understand – that *all objects have names.* That idea seems to us so obvious that it's hard to realize that we once did not know it. But lots of babies who are developing quite normally start to point *before* they understand this.

- So a fourth great benefit of pointing is that you can do it effectively even when you don't yet know that objects have names – whereas both sign language and spoken language need that knowledge first.

One more reason. Once ordinary babies start to point, they don't just do it in order to be given the object. They find that people often name the object at the same time as giving it: 'Yes, here's your teddy!' or 'A drink?' So they begin to learn that objects do have different names, and they may even start to point just to hear the name. Sometimes they will point and say 'Da?' or 'What dat?' or even 'Dat duck?' For some children with autism, the penny will drop in just the same way, and they get enthusiastic about pointing in order to hear the name; for others it takes longer, but they are still beginning to understand that things have names, and therefore beginning to be ready for words, whether signed or spoken.

- So the fifth reason to teach pointing is that it prepares the child for real words and a varied vocabulary.

PRACTICAL STEPS IN TEACHING POINTING

Children with autism differ from each other in all sorts of ways, just as other children do. They have different personalities and different rates of development, even though they share a diagnosis.

This means that it is quite difficult to write a 'How to Do It' guide that will be suitable for every child. This chapter is therefore written in a series of steps. As you read it, think about what stage your child has reached already, or whether you still need to teach at particular stages. For instance, are you sure whether he yet knows that objects have names? Or is he perhaps not yet reaching for things at all?

If you are not sure whether he has reached a certain stage or not, probably he still needs a little practice at that level before you can move him on to the next stage.

At each step you are trying to get to the stage at which your child has become so used to this new action that he does it *spontaneously*, without being told or shown. But do remember that *all* the steps are difficult for a child with autism, and that each step takes time. Marc Segar, an adult with autism, has written that 'Autistic people have to understand scientifically what non-autistic people already understand instinctively', and this is true of every individual step of learning to communicate. The way parents tend to put it is that they have had to deliberately teach their child every new communication skill. So don't be surprised if once you have taught your child to do certain things spontaneously, you still have to remind him quite often. This is just the way it is in autism.

Let's start with what most parents say when they're asked whether their young child with autism can point.

> *I've tried over and over again to show him how to point. He just takes no notice of me.*

Most parents expect their child to imitate them, and to take pleasure in doing so. But children with autism usually don't have the urge to imitate actions (though some may echo sounds). This is partly because they don't identify with someone else in a social way, so

the only reason why they might imitate is just to make a toy work. Pointing is not something like making a toy work, so they don't 'see the point of pointing'.

We could point in front of our child for weeks or months, and he still wouldn't see why he should do the same. So somehow we need to *help him to experience for himself* what pointing feels like *and* why it is useful.

Let's assume three things about your child:

- he's reached 18 months or more without pointing

- he does use his forefinger (probably with his thumb) for picking up tiny objects such as raisins or bits of chocolate
- he does reach for things he wants that he can see just above his grasp.

(If these three things are *not* true of your child, we shall be coming back shortly to what you should do.)

We need to make him aware of his forefinger as a 'special' finger

Forefingers normally become 'special' at about 11 months in two different ways, and in each case this is because the child's physical development now allows her to use the forefinger separately from her other fingers, in a way she couldn't do properly before:

- she can pick up tiny objects in a 'pincer grip', using thumb and forefinger opposite each other
- she can use her forefinger to point.

Children with autism may not be delayed at all in the pincer grip, which is not a social skill; but they will usually be very delayed in the social skill of pointing. (Some children with autism do point non-socially and without meaning, and we'll come back to that.)

Touch-pointing and distance-pointing

There are two sorts of pointing, and we need to encourage both. Touch-pointing is when a child touches an object with his forefinger, rather than the whole hand; the most obvious example is when you show a child a picture book and he touches objects in the picture as you name them, or touches the picture of the cow as you say 'moo!'

Touch-pointing usually comes first, because it is less abstract. It's a helpful way of the child becoming more aware of his forefinger because he *feels* the touch at the tip of his finger. If it's not happening naturally, you can give him this experience.

If he will look through a book or illustrated catalogue with you (beside you on the couch if he tends to wriggle off your knee), encourage this – perhaps when he is a little sleepy, when many children are more tolerant. As he puts his hand on the picture, find a way to take his hand and curl his other fingers under (into his palm) so that only the forefinger touches the picture. Do it gently and quickly so that he doesn't object, but press the finger to the page so that he is aware of using it, then let go. You can have this picture-session daily to give him lots of practice – make it as game-like and fun as you can. Most children enjoy animal noises still more than words.

You can do the same thing in a game of touch-pointing and naming parts of his and your face; remember that at this stage it is more important that he should touch-point than name.

Try having small objects around him that he might like to pick up; think carefully beforehand and choose whatever is tempting to him. Some of them may be food. As his hand goes to pick one up, again curl his fingers underneath so that only the forefinger is left stretched out, touch the forefinger to the object, and *then* let him pick it up. If possible the forefinger should be quite tightly stretched, to give him the 'body-memory' of the touch. Name the object yourself if you like, but don't expect *him* to.

You will probably get very quick and neat about curling his fingers under so that only his forefinger is touching what he wants, and then letting him take it, without getting too much in his way. You want him to tolerate this, so don't allow it to become a struggle;

find a calmer time if you have any problems. What you are aiming at is that it will become a *habit* to touch-point as he reaches, so that it begins to feel natural to him. Of course, it is not very natural to point in this situation, but you are preparing him for the next, still more important stage of distance-pointing. You can move on as soon as he is reasonably tolerant of you curling his fingers on a regular basis.

Distance-pointing is both a more abstract and a more social gesture, since he will eventually be using it to ask for your help.

This time, choose some more objects that will attract him, and that he can easily see when they are at a little distance from him. Some might be objects that he holds or twiddles a bit obsessionally; some might be sparkly or visually fascinating objects; some might be favourite toys or food. Put these around the room where he can see them but not reach them (but not so far away that he would be too discouraged to reach).

Wait for him to reach for one. The moment he does, take his hand and form a point with the forefinger (not touching the thing); use his name to say (for instance) '*Daniel pointing!*' and immediately give him what he pointed at. This should all happen too quickly for him to object to you – so quickly that he almost thinks he pointed and you responded to him. This is what you are aiming for – that he *gets the experience of what you really want him to do spontaneously.* What is more, he discovers from that experience that pointing is a specially good way of getting the things he wants.

Giving your child what he points for as often as possible is really important (though obviously you can't give him the moon or an aeroplane!). He needs to learn pointing as a *meaningful gesture.* You can make pointing happen *meaningfully* many times each day; and if he is at nursery or school, perhaps they could do it the same way too. It is giving your child access to what he pointed for that makes it meaningful in his eyes; sometimes this means opening a door or giving him a push on the swing rather than actually handing him an object. Don't forget to use his name in telling him in a pleased voice what he has done: '*Daniel pointing!*' – you are going to build on this later.

Some children take longer than others to make this connection, and even longer to point reliably and spontaneously. It's well worth persisting, though, because the child at last has a way of communicating, and realizes this; and that gives him a good basis for moving on.

As your child gets more used to pointing and is beginning to do it spontaneously, don't pounce on him too quickly – give him space to point for himself. Now you can try saying to him, if he forgets,

'Daniel – pointing!' This is why you gave him this word earlier – so that you could remind him.

Occasionally you may find that your child begins to echo the word 'pointing', sometimes without actually pointing himself. If that happens, he is beginning to be ready for words as well. Persevere with the pointing gesture, but *extend his echoing to make it more conversational* – say 'Yes – pointing to the *cup*', or whatever it is.

Pointing for choosing

A good way of helping your child to practice pointing (both touch and distance) is to let him choose *which* he wants out of two things. This can happen many times a day in ordinary situations, and is partly a matter of remembering to offer him a choice whenever you can, rather than just offering one thing.

Apart from giving him extra opportunities for pointing, getting your child used to making choices will give him more of a sense of being able to *negotiate with you*, and this is likely to improve his understanding of what communication is for. *Achieving negotiation will be one of your top priorities for the quality of his communication.*

Ordinary ways in which you might want to give him choice will easily arise during mealtimes. You could pour a mug of orange juice and one of milk, and ask '*orange* or *milk*?' Emphasize each word separately, while you yourself can either point to each as you say it, or (if you have a mug in each hand) push each forward a little, in time with the word. Or you could use the milk-carton and the orange-bottle, so long as they are easy to tell apart. Then wait for him to point, and instantly reward him with his choice. If he doesn't point, try to offer again; don't give up too easily! Obviously, whether he touch-points or distance-points will depend on how far away you are holding the drinks.

He does need to be doing some spontaneous pointing in order for this to work, since it is not easy to shape his hand while you are holding the two choices. It is a useful thing to do when he is ready to be *reminded* by your own pointing. Or if he is not quite at that stage, you *might* get another person to help you, so that one person is offering the choices while the other (from behind the child) shapes his hand, trying not to be too obtrusive so as not to put him off. You may find it *easier*, in this case, for the child to be on the 'shaper's' lap.

This is just one example of a common choice; but there's no limit to the possibilities. For instance, you could wait for a choice between 'honey or jelly?', 'this book or that book?', 'apple or banana?', or whatever is right for your child. Even if you know the likely answer, still give your child the choice.

Expand this to other situations. What about 'blue socks or green socks?', 'this toy or that toy?', 'Thomas Tank or Postman Pat?' You will begin to find yourself thinking about ways to offer choices that are clear-cut: for instance, offering a choice of cereal in little variety-pack boxes. If you are lucky, you may also find that giving him choices reduces tantrums.

So he's pointing – but it doesn't look quite natural

The finger point is not a complete gesture in itself when children develop it naturally. Ordinary children point, *look at you (making eye-contact)* and *make a sound (or word)* as a three-part complex gesture. For a child with autism, we need to teach this complex gesture bit

by bit. Remember that true eye-contact means looking at your eyes (*sharing* a look), not just at your body.

Once again, you might wait a long time before your child discovers how to make eye-contact when he points. So you make that experience happen for him. Once he has got the idea of pointing, put your face in line with his eyes so that *you* are making the eye-contact, as best you can – sometimes it *will* be difficult, because he may try to avoid this. *Persevere* – because *pointing is not a real gesture unless it is a message for someone*, and looking at you is what *shows that it is a message for you.* Giving him what he pointed for now rewards him for both the point and the look together – so wait a second until you get the look that you are helping him with.

He may begin by giving you that look because he is surprised that you are not giving him the object that he now expects to get when he points, but soon he will get used to pointing and looking almost simultaneously.

Now you could go on to the *third part of the gesture* – the *sound or word.* You may need to reduce the number of objects you use at this stage, so as not to confuse your child with too many words at first, especially if he has no other words yet.

As you give him the object he has pointed for, and make eye-contact, name the object very clearly: 'It's a *drink*'; 'It's a *ball*'. Decide beforehand on what words you are going to use, especially if more than one person is teaching him, and especially if some of his favourite objects don't have an obvious name (for instance a '*flapper*' or a '*twiddler*'). You need to be consistent at this stage.

Again, wait a second to give your child time to respond. You want him to imitate your word eventually, but he may not manage this for a while. Be satisfied with just a sound at first, which may be no more than an imitation of your mouth movement, with no voice behind it. Gradually, the sound will probably get more and more like the main sound in the word you are using, and even like the word itself. Take it at his pace and don't overload him – none of this is easy for him.

Don't forget, too, that there are some children with especially severe speech difficulties who will not manage to speak, however hard we try. For those children we shall be looking for alternatives as they show how hard it is for them. But *every* child will be given their best chance of speech by giving them the experience of the power of pointing. Children with autism, like other children, can make a leap forward in their understanding of communication through this experience.

COPING WITH LESS STRAIGHTFORWARD SITUATIONS

Should I teach my child pointing if he already uses some words – does he need pointing as well?

Yes. Pointing (especially when you add eye-contact) is especially useful for giving the child a framework or structure for 'shared attention' and 'shared understanding'. For ordinary babies, one of their most valuable social experiences is to look at or listen to something and then share their interest with another person. Shared *interest* then quickly becomes shared *understanding* – and it is no exaggeration to say that *shared understanding is the cornerstone of communication.*

Children with autism often have understanding without sharing it. Pointing and giving eye-contact makes the sharing more clear and obvious to them than words can.

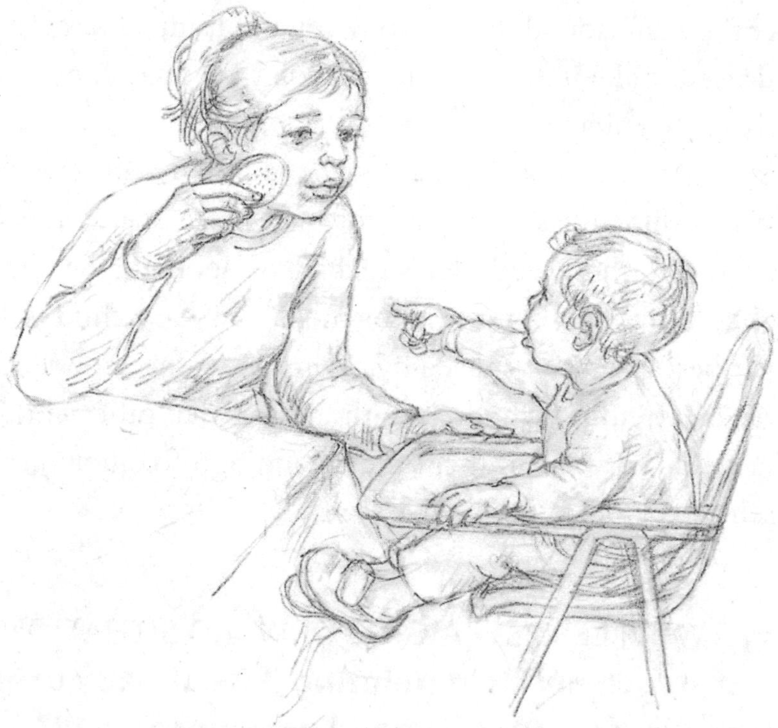

What if my child is already pointing, but doesn't seem to know why he's doing it or what it means?

Some children who have been taught to point, without making sure that they get what they point for, learn to *put their finger in that position* but not why. For these children, it is as if they have learned just another mannerism like hand-flapping or finger-flicking, and this is not helpful to them because it has nothing to do with communication.

There are also some children who are fascinated by imitation itself, and imitate actions they see on TV or from people, including pointing, without trying to make sense of them. This is a skill that can be made useful to them, by making it more meaningful, but it is not very useful *until* it has become meaningful.

If your child is pointing without meaning, you will need to spend quite a lot of time emphasizing the meaning (the reward) in the ways we have already described. You will also need to emphasize the *social* aspects of touch-pointing; for instance, choose an animal picture-book, and spend time going through it with your child, pointing at the animals, waiting for him to do so in imitation (or shaping his hand to do so) and making the animal noise as a reward. The social aspect is especially important for children who point meaninglessly, since they have learned to point in an especially solitary way, and need to unlearn this.

Often you will find that you cannot see what your child is pointing at. In fact, this is what tells you that he doesn't know what he is doing – the point has nothing to do with wanting something. Ignore these undirected points, but give him plenty of opportunity to reach for things, and shape the reach into a point in the usual way, rewarding him *only* when you can see his wish to get the object.

It is *always* difficult to *unlearn* things, but you will succeed if you persevere.

What if my child is under 18 months?

Active pointing usually develops at about 11–12 months and, as we've said, comes at the same time as the ability to pick up tiny objects between finger and thumb. It may be that your child is just generally a bit delayed, rather than specifically delayed in communication. Look to see whether he can use finger and thumb to pick up raisins for example. If he *can* do this, but not point (and if he is also not following your points), then he is communication-delayed, and you can try the methods already given; but don't forget that he is still very young, and may be very intolerant, so don't push him too hard. If he is behind in *all* uses of his forefinger, then you will need to take extra time for making him aware of his forefinger as a 'special' finger, helping him to separate it from the others for picking things up as well as touch-pointing.

Giving practice to the slow forefinger

Like anything else, this will work better if it's fun! Try to make everything into a game, or rewarding in some other way.

You're trying to find ways to give your child a richer experience of his forefinger, both on its own and in relation to his thumb. Try the following:

- In lap play, or in the quieter moments of rough and tumble play, stimulate each of his forefingers on its own, in whatever ways he will let you. Tickle and flick his finger with your own forefinger, touch it to your lips as you blow raspberries, nibble it, blow on the tip, let him wobble your nose with it. You may find you get good eye-contact during this, which is a bonus; many children with autism give eye-contact during rough and tumble, but it is much closer to real conversation when it happens during the quiet intervals.

- Make these activities into a little ritual game by adding a nonsense song to what you are doing – for instance 'Tikki, tikki, tikki – puh, puh, puh' as you flick his finger with yours and then put it to your lips. Or use his forefinger across your lips to make an 'Indian war cry' type of noise.

(We're now getting closer to the interactive play that is described in another chapter.)

- Mix wallpaper paste with a little water-paint, spread it on paper, and shape his hand in yours to make his forefinger draw lines and squiggles – or use finger paints. Similarly, draw his finger through other textures such as damp sand or even plaster of Paris. When the plaster has set with his finger-marks still in it, he will probably enjoy trailing his finger through the channel he made, fingering the holes, or pushing edible balls such as aniseed balls along the channels with one finger. Let him scratch his nail along surfaces like sandpaper. Make a little 'book' of highly textured paper or cloth.
- In the bath: blow bubbles and show him how to pop them with one finger; let the tap trickle into a small funnel and show him how he can put his finger on the end of the tube to stop the flow; let him scrape marks in the softened soap.

- Using a saucer with sugar crystals in it, damp his forefinger and show him how he can pick up and eat the sugar (or try with tiny crumbs of cake – whatever he likes best), just by touching with the damp finger.
- Play games using your own finger and thumb to '*peck*' at things – make funny bird noises as you do so. See if he will let you make his finger and thumb peck in the same way, or do it himself. Try sticking a small coloured label on the finger nail, to emphasize the forefinger.
- He might now be ready to pick things up with finger and thumb. Make sure the food morsels you scatter are too small to pick up with clustered fingers, and that he likes the way they taste.

Once he is using his forefinger independently, he is ready to move on to pointing. If he still needs more forefinger practice, think up more things that he might enjoy fingering – the chapter on *Sharing Conceptual Play* may help you.

What if my child just never reaches for things?

You do need reaching in order to shape the whole-hand reach into a point. Think about *why* your child isn't reaching.

It might be because he is very fascinated with one or two things (such as door-swinging or spinning trike-wheels) and doesn't want other objects. It might be that he is very passive and uninterested in any play, or just runs to and fro. Perhaps he doesn't like the effort involved in extending his arm.

Once you have thought about what is the likely reason, you will need to experiment in order to tempt him to reach for things that are convenient for your purpose. If he swings doors, you could lock the door for a while so that he has to find something else to swing, and then try him with cardboard books, paper to flap and little cars with opening doors, or a ball on a string.

All of these give a similar visual sensation, and you could even try an old catalogue or telephone book. If he spins trike wheels, put the trike right away and show him other, smaller things to spin, like tops and lids, and wheels on toy cars. Look around for visual and light-reflecting objects: holographic plastic toys, plastic slinky, a small torch or a string of shiny metal buttons. Tempt him away from his running, even if you think you are giving him a new fascination – some fascinations can be more constructive than others, and worth having if they can be built on.

If you do think your child is not reaching out because of pure passivity, you could try getting him used to the idea during rough and tumble play; you will probably be able to bring his arms in and out in that setting, without his objecting, so that he experiences a 'passive stretch'. You can also start by putting the things he might want quite close, so that he doesn't have to reach far. Very gradually increase the distance over two or three weeks.

Shouldn't I be teaching him to follow my point as well?

Yes, and you are already giving him practice when you look at a book with him and touch-point at pictures. Following a point usually develops first (before pointing) in ordinary babies. The trouble is that it's much more difficult to *make this happen*, than it is to make pointing happen.

You will be most successful if you point at something that really stands out against an empty background: for instance, an aeroplane, a bird, or a hot-air balloon against the sky. Or you could try pointing at something that he's already staring at, such as street lights against a dark background. You will need to put your arm close to the side of his head, so that he can peer along the arm and beyond your pointing finger.

One problem is that many children with autism have real difficulty picking out what they are looking for against a busy background, even if they are trying; so you might not be very successful until much later, when you can give him more verbal clues where to look. Do remember that it is far more important for him to learn to point himself, since that gives him true communicative power.

You will probably have noticed that some of the activities suggested in this chapter could be quite a lot of fun for both your child and yourself. 'Teaching pointing' might sound a rather serious business; but if you try to keep it light-hearted, it will help your child to find real enjoyment in playing with you even before he succeeds in learning to point. Once he does start pointing with meaning, he's likely to get much more interested in other experiences that he might get from you, and look to you more actively for entertainment and interaction. One family were so impressed at their child's enjoyment of the 'conversations' he had through pointing, that they pasted up magazine pictures all over his bedroom wall, so that he could point at these too, and gradually name them. And this became his next major step forward – he wasn't just pointing to get things, but *pointing in order to comment.*

Trying to comment makes a child much more a part of his family's social world, and this is our hope for you and your child at this stage.

7 UNDERSTANDING LANGUAGE

INTRODUCTION

Children with autism usually have considerable difficulty in making sense of spoken language. They also find it hard to understand body language, including gestures and facial expressions. Other children naturally use people's body language as extra clues to help them understand and learn words. Being unaware or unsure of the meaning of both spoken language and body language must make other people very confusing for a child with autism.

It is very common for the people closest to a child to think that his understanding is better than it really is. Some children are clever at finding extra clues in objects, actions and situations, or remembering a common sequence of events, so that they may *appear* to understand more language than they actually do. For example, your child may see you pick up his bath-towel and pyjamas, and he knows he is going to have a bath. Then, when you say 'Come on, it's bath-time', it *seems* that he has understood your words. This is fine when the child is in those familiar situations. However, the trouble with thinking he understood when he didn't is that it can lead people to expect too much of him in other situations, where he really doesn't understand what is going on or why something is happening.

Using *simpler* words and phrases with extra clues to explain something, negotiate with or direct the child, can often help him to feel more confident and secure, and can even be the solution to what seemed to be a 'behaviour problem'. For example, if one day you tell your child 'It's bath-time', *without* picking up the towel and pyjamas first, he may seem to ignore or 'disobey' you. He might even have a tantrum when he does not understand what is going on, or why you seem to be getting cross with him. If you explain and *show him* what you mean, and *help him* to 'cooperate' at these times, then over the weeks or months, with lots of repetition, he is more likely to learn to understand what the words actually mean.

The nature of autism means that it may be almost impossible to work out exactly how much your child *can* understand. A language test often doesn't help: the child's responses may be inconsistent from one day to the next, or what he does in the assessment situation may not be the same as he would do in a more familiar setting. This is because children with autism don't realize that you are supposed to try hard in a test! They only try if you catch their interest, they only concentrate for as long as they want to at the time, and they may not see the point of cooperating, even in a play-based assessment.

The intention of this chapter is to increase your awareness and insight, so that you can help your child make sense of *more* of what you say to him, and of the social world around him. This may involve giving him extra 'clues', such as objects, pictures and gestures or signs, using simple repetitive language yourself, and making some situations more predictable.

First, it may help to consider how *we* feel when we can't understand something, and what might help.

WHAT'S IT LIKE, NOT TO UNDERSTAND EASILY WHAT OTHER PEOPLE ARE SAYING?

We have all had experience of some of these situations:

- If we hear people speaking in a totally unfamiliar language, we tend to 'switch off' and very quickly stop listening.
- If we know a few words in that language, we may work harder to listen for those words and try to make sense of what is being said. This is very tiring, and hard to keep up for more than a few minutes.
- Even hearing *our* own language spoken with a strong regional accent different from our own can make it very hard to follow and understand.
- When people use specialized words (for instance medical or computer jargon), we may have great difficulty following the conversation. We may 'tune out' and give up listening.
- If we know it is really important to take in information, or if we start to worry about looking 'stupid', we might

begin to feel anxious. Anxiety makes it even harder to concentrate, understand and remember.

WHAT HELPS US TO UNDERSTAND?

In all the above examples, the speaker might be able to help us understand more. For example, they could:

- speak more slowly and clearly
- use shorter, simpler sentences
- repeat or rephrase parts of what they have said
- use gesture or mime to illustrate key words
- use clear facial expressions and dramatic tones of voice, to get across the mood and emotion of what they are saying
- show an object or picture as they say a certain word
- draw a diagram or map to clarify something
- jot down some key points in writing that we can look at afterwards.

Above all, it helps if the speaker *knows* that we are having difficulty, so that he or she can give us the clues that we will find most useful, taking into account our age, experience and knowledge. Some of the above ways of helping may be especially useful for particular children with autism. It's our job to find which ones work best for each child.

HOW DO ORDINARY CHILDREN LEARN TO UNDERSTAND LANGUAGE?

Usually, babies are *naturally interested* in people, and what they do and say. They *watch* faces and actions, *listen* to different voices, take *an interest in routines* such as dressing, bathing and mealtimes, and enter into little games and 'conversations' without words from a very early age (see chapter on *Interactive Play*). This helps them to get familiar with and make sense of other people's gestures, facial expressions and behaviour, long before they understand actual words.

These everyday games and routines are often accompanied by language that is simple and repetitive, with exaggerated intonation, and often timed to fit in exactly with the actions.

For example:

> A parent may lift a baby up and swing or slide her down playfully, to a repeated chant of 'Up up up and down you go!'
>
> When finishing a meal, they might say something like, 'One more spoon – *in* it goes. In – in – *in*!'
>
> And at bath-time: 'Let's wash that *tummy*. Here goes – wash your *tummy*!'

As the ordinary baby hears these words and phrases often, and in a familiar context, she gradually learns that there is a *link* between the sounds she hears and the objects or actions they refer to. By the age of about a year, she realizes that *people and objects have names*, and that she can find them out by pointing, looking and vocalizing in a questioning way. She also learns to link words and phrases with *simple actions*, and may enjoy the reaction she gets when she responds to 'clap hands' or 'where's your nose?', or does an action that goes with a favourite song. In this way she starts to build up a *receptive vocabulary* (words that she *receives* or understands): she will always understand far more words than she actively uses.

In these early stages, young children latch on to single *key words* in the language around them: those that they hear spoken with emphasis, or that are particularly meaningful or rewarding. Sometimes little *phrases* are learned as whole units: for example, a baby who responds to 'clap hands' by doing the action does not necessarily understand the word 'hand' when it's said on its own.

The ordinary development of understanding, or *comprehension* as it is called when talking about language, is a long and complex process. It is difficult to be sure exactly how it happens, and the path will be a little different for each child. However, over several years many things have to be combined (not necessarily in this order):

- The child actively works at making sense of people and the things they do and say, so that familiar words and phrases gradually *take on meaning* for her, when earlier they were more like 'background music' to everyday routines and games.

- She makes use of what she can see (*visual clues*) to help her understand what is going on, and to help her learn *new words* as they crop up, in situations that are meaningful to her.

- She begins to grasp *early concepts* and the language that goes with them – for example the idea that things can *disappear* ('gone!') and be found again ('there!'); that things can be different *sizes* ('big' and 'little') and move in different *directions* ('up' and 'down'); that there can be different *amounts* of things ('one', 'two', 'lots'), and so on.

- As her *memory* grows, she actively wants to know the names of more things and what words mean. She can 'ask' for this information by making eye-contact, pointing and vocalizing, and later by using words such as 'That?' or 'Wassat?' in a questioning tone of voice.
- Her *receptive vocabulary* (the range of words she understands) increases to include more words for actions and activities, places, positions and descriptions, and generally more

'abstract' ideas (like 'soon' or 'nice') than the first few words she understood.

- Early on, she will have picked out one *key word* in a sentence that she recognized and understood. For example, understanding just *one* word ('upstairs' or 'bath'), may be enough (combined with seeing you getting ready), for her to cooperate with: 'Let's go upstairs now because it's time for your bath.' At later stages, she will be able to take in and understand two and then more key words (and eventually *all* the words in a sentence), without relying on extra visual clues.

- By *combining* her greater receptive vocabulary, memory and knowledge about the world, the ordinary toddler is able to *generalize* what she has learned: that is, she applies what she knows from her own past experience, to help her make sense of new situations and the language that goes with them.

ATTENTION

The first point made in the last section was that babies are naturally interested in people and the things they do and say. A child's *attention skills* are fundamental to the whole process of learning to understand language. This involves both *looking at* and *listening to* the adults who take care of and play with him or her, in order to take in the language that goes with everyday activities. For children with autism, several things may interfere with their attention, and distract them from this vital process:

- Children with autism often seem *to lack that basic interest in people.* It is well known that they make much less eye-contact (*sharing* a look with someone) than other children: this in itself makes it hard to get a game or conversation going.

- They seem to have *difficulty making sense* of the way adults talk to them from a very early age: not just the words, but the *whole of 'conversation'*, with its finely timed two-way flow, eye-contact and other social signals. (See chapter on *Interactive Play*.) They do not easily learn the meaning of facial expressions, gestures and other body language. Because these things do not make sense, the child takes less notice of people and misses out even more.

- They seem to have *other priorities and preoccupations* in life that can take a lot of time and attention away from social play. For example, some children find objects far more interesting than people, and many are deeply fascinated by visual patterns or movements, such as lines of objects or wheels going round.

- They may be unable to let you know that they feel unwell, worried, in a bad mood or excited about something else, and therefore *can't concentrate* on your words.

- Some children with autism experience *what their senses tell them* in a different or 'distorted' way, which distracts them further from the need to make sense of other people. For instance, they may be very sensitive to certain textures, so that the feel of certain clothing or seating is uncomfortable or even painful. The particular pitch of a buzzing light or machine might be unbearable to some children, or the

hum might simply be more interesting than an adult trying to play, who is making faces and sounds that confuse the child.

- Some people with autism seem to get *overstimulated or overwhelmed* by the sights and sounds of everyday life. If your child is like this, a visit to a busy place such as a supermarket or a party might be really distressing for him; it might be impossible for him to attend to what you are saying, even if you are trying to comfort or reassure him with your words.

Children with autism *do* of course interact with their parents and carers, usually 'on their own terms', and around anything that interests and makes sense to them. Active physical (or 'rough and tumble') play is often one of the best situations for this. Some may well pick up and understand some of the most common words used repetitively around them. However, they will almost certainly have much *less* experience than other children of *listening to and making sense of the language that goes alongside everyday activities.* They also tend not to enjoy those little moments of quiet exchange of sounds, movements and facial expressions that we think of as 'baby chat'.

SPOKEN LANGUAGE

In addition, most children with autism seem to have a particular difficulty with language itself. In the early stages, they may find it much harder than other children to make firm *links* between the *sounds or words they hear*, and the *objects or actions they refer to*; and they have still more difficulty guessing at the *intentions of the person speaking*. Children who are good at using visual clues might sometimes make *mistakes* because they have not made these links. For example, if you are holding your child's clean towel and pyjamas after doing the washing, and you say, 'I'm just taking these upstairs', he may think it is bath-time and get very confused.

Many children with autism *don't simply 'pick up'* new words and their meanings from everyday life, but need to be taught them specifically. Some don't seem to realize that things have names (see chapter on *Teaching Pointing*), so they don't get into that social game of 'asking' what things are, which helps ordinary children to increase their receptive vocabulary. Even if they do, they might 'collect' names of a narrow range of things that are of particular interest to them, but not so useful in everyday life and conversation (such as the names of all the trains in 'Thomas the Tank Engine' or makes of cars).

Children with autism vary in how easily they grasp *early concepts* and the language that goes with them. Those who have additional learning disabilities are of course likely to take longer, and they need more help to learn and remember new ideas, even if they are motivated and attending. Some children will be able to demonstrate quickly that they understand certain concepts; they may sort, match and stack objects, or operate the computer or DVD. But they still may need to be taught specifically to understand the *associated words*, such as 'same', 'smaller', 'rewind' and so on.

Even if your child can use and understand some whole sentences, he will still probably need extra help with understanding particular words and concepts. Children with autism are often confused by certain aspects of language. For example:

- There can be two words for the same thing, such as 'beach' and 'seaside', 'rabbit' and 'bunny'.
- A word can have two or more meanings, such as 'soft' meaning quiet, soft to touch, or silly.
- Children as they begin to read may be confused when two words can sound the same but have different spellings as well as different meanings, such as 'sea' and 'see', 'here' and 'hear'.
- Some words 'change' according to who is involved and how: such as the grammatical pronouns 'he', 'she', 'I' and 'you'.

- At the 'top end' of the ability scale, some children with autism understand and use a lot of language rather inflexibly; so they are very confused by jokes, puns, sarcasm and figures of speech, and will need careful explanation. These children are often described as having *Asperger syndrome.*

One difficulty that all children with autism share to some degree, is in *generalizing* what they have learned – that is, using concepts in a whole range of situations. This is very important in language development. For example, a child who understands the word 'coat' has to learn that it refers to coats of all different sizes, colours, styles and types, not just his own particular one. The ability to generalize depends on *flexible* thinking and learning, especially when it comes to words and concepts that have different meanings in different contexts. For example, a *big* dog is small compared with a *small* elephant! This kind of flexibility can be particularly hard for people with autism.

As we've said, some children are very good at using visual clues in objects, actions and situations, to help them understand what is going on, when they don't understand all or some of the words being used. This can make them *appear* to understand more language than they actually do.

Another reason for adults thinking a child understands more than he really does, is to do with '*echolalia*' (echoed speech). Young children whose language is developing normally do go through a stage of echoing (or copying) adult speech, but many children with autism echo much more and for much longer. Sometimes, echoing a question can indicate that the child has not understood it, or that he doesn't know how to answer it; and echoing his mother's 'you' ('Do you want a drink?') may lead him to refer to himself as 'you' ('You want a drink'). But some children with autism actually seem to learn to use language by picking up and remembering whole 'chunks' from adults' speech, or from books, DVDs, television advertisements and computer games. They may even be able to remember these phrases or sentences and use them quite appropriately at other times.

The relevance of this to your child's understanding is that *he may say things that he can't understand himself.* But the usual pattern of language development is that children always understand more words than they actively use. We are used to assuming that if a child says something, he can understand those words. With a child who echoes this may not be true, because he has learned the phrase or sentence as a whole unit, without understanding every part.

HOW MIGHT DIFFICULTIES IN UNDERSTANDING LANGUAGE AFFECT YOUR CHILD'S BEHAVIOUR?

We have already discussed that when we have trouble understanding what people are saying, we may 'switch off' or 'tune out', stop listening, and feel a range of emotions, such as boredom, anxiety, confusion or frustration. Children react in individual ways to these feelings, and to situations where they don't understand what is going on.

Sometimes children with autism get agitated and seem to feel pressurized, maybe behaving in disturbing ways, such as hurting themselves or others. They may take refuge in a 'favourite' repetitive activity or movement, which can be their way of coping with feeling anxious. Sometimes they have a 'glazed' or distant expression, and just seem to ignore what is being said. Or they might withdraw physically from the people around them, moving away to be on their own.

WHAT *DOES* YOUR CHILD UNDERSTAND?

Obviously, the question about understanding language is not a simple 'yes or no' one, as in 'Does he understand English?' Speech and language therapists sometimes use tests to find out more about a child's comprehension 'level'. These usually involve asking the child to point to pictures, or to do specific tasks with toys or objects. But formal language tests, even those based on play with toys, are often not very helpful for assessing children with autism. This is partly because they depend on the child being both able and willing to attend and cooperate. As we've seen, children with autism also tend to learn in a less flexible way than other children, and find it hard to apply what they know to different situations, including test situations.

The aim of this section is to show you how you can make use of everyday situations and activities, to help you get an idea of your child's level of understanding. For example, he may be at a stage where he really does not understand words at all, but is relying on familiar routines and visual clues. He may be understanding a small number of familiar key words. On the other hand he may have a large 'receptive vocabulary', but have difficulty taking in and remembering sentences with more than one key word. He may be at a much more advanced level, where he can follow instructions with two or three key words, answer simple questions, and often understand when you tell him what is happening: but even so, he will probably find it much harder to follow more *abstract ideas* such as question words (e.g. who, where, why) or things involving time (e.g. soon, yesterday, tomorrow).

To start with, we suggest that, for a day or two, you focus your mind on your child's understanding of language as you go about your everyday activities. You will need to notice what sorts of sentences you and other people use when talking to him, and how he responds in different situations. It may help to jot down some examples of things he has responded to correctly, being aware of any clues he could be using to help him understand – something like this:

What I said	*Clues*
Get your shoes	Just had his socks put on
Where's your coat?	Saw me pick up my keys
Do you want a drink?	Heard the rustle of a juice being pulled

Then, to check out whether your child understands your *actual words*, you need to repeat these same sentences on another occasion *without the extra clues*. So another time you might ask him to get his shoes *before* putting on his socks. Or you might ask him if he wants a yogurt *before* you get them out, and see if he goes to where they are kept.

Once you have found some examples of words or sentences he *does* understand, you might try out some *variations* to find out what else he can understand.

For example: if he can get his shoes without extra clues, can he get other things that you ask for? If you find he can fetch all sorts of everyday objects, you might try making it slightly harder.

For example:

Can he fetch two things such as coat *and* shoes?

Can he fetch 'Daddy's coat' as well as his own?

Can he get something that's not in its usual place if you tell him where to find it? (Such as 'Get your coat – it's in the garden'.)

This kind of informal testing is not intended to 'trick' your child or to catch him out, but to make sure the people around him don't underestimate or overestimate his understanding. It will also help you to identify which kinds of clues help him the most.

When you say something to him that he doesn't understand, you might try to work out the reason why not:

- was he attending and listening in the first place?
- was there a particular word he didn't know?
- was the sentence too long or too complicated?

You could try simplifying it, breaking it up into two shorter phrases, or saying it in a slightly different way. For example, you might notice that when you are careful not to give any visual clues, he doesn't understand a sentence like:

'Don't you think it might be a good idea to put those away now, because we're going out soon?'

This is a very long and complex sentence, and yet parents do sometimes talk like this to young children – especially when they're trying to 'soften the blow' of having to clear up or stop doing something. You could see if he can understand either:

'Tim, let's put the bricks away', or

'Finished – bricks in the box'

and *then* tell him, 'Time to go out', checking out separately whether he understands each phrase.

Checking out your child's understanding within everyday activities might involve some of the following ideas, but you need to choose things that are particularly useful for his activities and your situation. For example:

> *Asking him where something is*, or to fetch or find something:
>
> e.g. 'Where's your cup?', 'Get your ball', 'Find teddy', 'Find Mummy's shoes'.
>
> *Asking him to do all sorts of different things*:
>
> e.g. 'Put your arms up', 'Come to mummy', 'Hang your coat up', 'Put it away', 'Put the apples in the bag',
>
> 'Give it to Mummy', 'Give Daddy the balloon'.
>
> *Asking him to show you something* when looking at pictures together:
>
> e.g. 'Where's the horse?' or 'Show me Thomas the Tank'.
>
> *Telling him not to do something:*
>
> e.g. 'Stop kicking', 'Don't sit on that!' or 'No splashing'.
>
> *Suggesting different actions* in play:
>
> e.g. 'Let's run!', 'Let's jump!' – or maybe actions within a song, such as 'This is the way we…*wash our hands*', or 'If you're happy and you know it…*touch your toes*' (giving him time to start the action before you do).
>
> *Telling him where something is* when you know he's looking for it:
>
> e.g. 'It's outside', 'on the chair', 'under the chair', 'in the kitchen', 'by the door', etc.

Offering him choices:

e.g. 'Do you want orange or milk?', 'A tickle or a swing?', 'Which one do you want?', 'Shall we go swimming or to the park?'

Asking him other sorts of questions:

'*Wh' questions* such as 'Who's that?', 'What do you want?', 'Where are you?', 'Which one?' ('When' and 'Why' questions are *much* more complicated to answer.)

'Yes/no' questions such as 'Have you got a tissue?', 'Does it hurt?', 'Is that nice?'

Other questions involving basic concepts such as 'How many?' or 'What colour?'

Telling him something that is going to happen:

e.g. 'It's dinner-time', 'We're going to see Granny', 'We have to wait here'.

This is *not* supposed to be a 'test' to work your way through, but to give you some starting-points. You could pick an example that you think is at about the right level, then follow our suggestions of *observing* your child's response; then checking out exactly which words and phrases he understands by:

- *simplifying* or saying it in a different way, if he clearly did *not* understand

- *cutting out clues* if he *did* respond correctly, to check that he understood the words

- *then* building up *variations* to find out which other words and ideas he can understand.

As well as establishing his level of comprehension, you may have discovered some of your child's *strengths,* such as visual skills, memory, or sequencing (putting things in order). These will be important for working out ways to help him move forward.

HOW CAN WE HELP A CHILD TO UNDERSTAND MORE LANGUAGE?

Unfortunately, we can't end this chapter with a simple list of 'what to do', or a step-by-step programme that would work for everyone! What follows is a series of ideas, pointers and guidelines for helping your child to understand more language, both in everyday situations and with regard to long-term learning. You may find it helpful to discuss particular ideas with your child's speech and language therapist, and any other professionals who are involved with him.

You will find that this part of the chapter overlaps with *The Beginnings of Structure.* Understanding language is an area where structure is especially important for children with autism, although not usually so necessary for other children.

Helping him to attend to your speech

One of the first priorities is to involve your child often in interactive *play,* so that your actions and words are really interesting and motivating to him. This will give him lots of opportunities to learn the basics of conversation, and to make a *habit of attending and listening* to you.

Make sure you have his attention when you speak to him. One way to be sure of getting *shared attention* is for *you* to join in with what *he* is interested in, and to talk about what he is already looking at or doing. (See *Interactive Play*.)

If he is involved in something, and you need to help him to *shift his attention* to listen to you, it may help to do any or all of the following:

- use his name at the beginning of a sentence (with a moment's pause after it, so he knows you're speaking to him)
- move to where he can see you easily, sitting or crouching down to his level
- touch him lightly
- take his hand as you start speaking
- cut down on distractions, by turning off the television or music, or perhaps removing a toy briefly, before speaking.

Being aware of your own language

It is important to monitor how *you* are using words as you speak to your child. If he is finding it hard to make sense of your speech, or seems to be ignoring you, you may be able to help by:

- using *shorter*, *simpler* phrases and sentences
- *repeating* your words a couple of times in a natural way
- *slowing* down your speech, so it is clearer (but not distorted)
- *emphasizing* key words

- *linking* your language (the words, timing and tone of voice) closely to what your child is doing or looking at, to help him make those vital connections between actions or objects and the words he hears
- *commenting* on his play and actions, so as to 'feed in' useful language about what he is attending to. It is very easy, when we are anxious about a child's communication, to slip into a pattern of directing and 'testing' him, and asking too many questions that he can't answer. It is fine to ask *some* questions of course, and to tell him what to do at times, but

he will also benefit from a simple commentary, which follows *his* interest

- *showing* him what you mean; for example by doing or helping him to do what you have asked, or by adding *visual clues* to your words, such as gestures, signs or pictures.

Using visual clues

An object, gesture, sign or picture can often help the child to *see what you mean*, and so understand your words more easily. This applies especially to those who clearly find *visual puzzles* (such as jigsaws, matching games and so on) much easier than communication.

In the section earlier, 'What *does* my child understand?' we discussed *cutting out* extra clues, but only in order to check out exactly what your child does and doesn't understand, and what seems to help. In everyday life we want to maximize his chances of understanding, by *using any clues that help him,* along with clear simple words.

There are several different kinds of visual clues. For example:

- We can *show the child an object as a clue* when we tell him what is happening: a towel for bath time, keys for going out, or a plate for dinner time. This is something many parents naturally do anyway. It can also be developed in a more systematic and planned way, where carefully chosen objects might be handed to the child, or put in a particular box or on a tray, as he is told that certain things are happening. This system is formally known as '*Objects of Reference*', because it uses objects that are connected with or *refer* to an activity. One of the advantages is that the object can be seen, felt and held, making a *clear 'bridge'* between the words and the activity or event.

- We can use a *clear consistent gesture* together with a key word or phrase: outstretched arms for 'come here', or miming drinking for 'milk' or 'juice'. Although many children with autism don't naturally seem to take in the clues from our usual body language, they *are* often helped by more systematically introducing gestures and *signs* (such as the Makaton vocabulary) to clarify key words as they are spoken. Signing should always involve using signs *with* speech, in order to *link* a sign with a word. In practice, signing key words has the added advantage of making adults speak more slowly and simply. As well as helping to get a child's attention, these signs can be a strong aid to learning and remembering words. They often help to make the meaning clearer, and of course a sign *lasts longer* than a spoken word, giving the child more time to take in what is being said.
- *Pictures*, whether photos or *symbols* (which are like simplified line drawings), can also be used to help a child understand what is being said. At first, you might just introduce one or two, such as a picture of the car or bus when you're going out, and one of the bath for bath-time. Later on, when he is familiar with several pictures, they can be used to show a *sequence of events*. For example, you may need to help him understand that he *can* do something he wants to, but something else has to happen first. So you might show him two pictures in sequence as you say, 'First put on your *socks*, then *dinner*', or 'First *shopping*, then the *park*'.

Some children really benefit from this idea of a sequence of pictures, which may eventually be expanded into a *visual timetable* to show a whole day's or week's events. It can help them understand what is happening, especially when there is a change in the usual routine and can so avoid a lot of distress and agitation. Supporting your spoken language with this kind of *visual structure* can really help a child to understand the words you are saying, and make things more predictable for him. There are more examples of this in the chapter on the *Beginnings of Structure.*

Teaching vocabulary

It will almost certainly be necessary to *teach the meaning of specific words* to your child as you notice gaps in his understanding. Again, it may be helpful to consult with any professionals involved, and agree on certain words or groups of words that will be especially useful to him and to you.

Some of the words you want him to understand will be about managing his basic needs, safety and behaviour in everyday situations. For example, he needs to understand 'no', 'stop', 'wait' or 'finished'. It will be much easier to help him through everyday activities such as dressing, eating or going out, if he can understand and respond to basic instructions like 'Come here', 'Sit down', 'Arms up', and so on. You may have to *show him* what you mean many times, and guide him physically, as well as using gestures or signs, before he actually understands these words and phrases.

However, learning to understand language, as we have seen, is a much bigger issue than simply learning to follow instructions. Your child also needs to understand words that help him *make sense of the world,* and to *understand the things people do and say* and to negotiate.

It is important to teach him words for things that interest and motivate *him*, as well as the ones *you* need him to learn.

- If your child is at a stage where he *wants* to sit with you, looking at books and pictures, then you might find you can teach him new words in a fairly traditional or 'formal' way. He may also enjoy picture lotto, and matching or sorting games, where there are lots of chances for you to teach him new words. However, many young children with autism are *not* motivated to learn in this way in the early years. There are plenty of other ways to help them learn to understand more words.

- Even if a child is not actively 'asking' for names of things (perhaps by pointing), we can make sure he hears the words for things that interest him, by commenting on his play and actions. For example, we may name his favourite toys as he picks up each one, chant 'round and round' as he spins something, and talk about 'splashing', 'water' and the names of body parts in the swimming pool or the bath ('splashing with your *hand*...splashing with your *foot*').

- Children can also learn a lot of language through *nursery rhymes*, *songs*, *finger plays*, and little spontaneous repetitive games or '*play routines*' (see *Interactive Play*). In children's songs, for example, the words are often very repetitive and simple, and do match the timing of the actions exactly. We can model the actions and guide the child to respond to the words, helped by the rhythm and tune, in a relaxed and enjoyable atmosphere. It is worth giving some thought to which songs and rhymes have *words that may be useful to your child*. For example, most of the words in 'Humpty Dumpty' will not mean much to your child, but if he enjoys a big tumble on the word '*fall*', then he probably will learn to understand *that* word, with a lot of repetition. Many other songs give opportunities to learn action words, body parts, animals, and so on: these can be excellent ways to add to your child's receptive vocabulary, although he may well need extra help to 'generalize' them.

Generalizing

Helping your child to apply what he has learned to other situations may need your special attention. You can't assume that because he understands the word 'cow' in his book, he will be able to show you the cow in a field; and even if he understands 'wait' while you pour his drink, he may not understand it at the supermarket check-out. You will need to make some allowances for his 'rigid' ways of learning and remembering, find ways around his inflexibility, and help him make connections in lots of different situations.

FINALLY

The process of learning to understand language is very complex, and for most of us continues for many years. Each child follows an individual path, depending on his or her own interests and experience. Children with autism usually need extra help on this journey. We hope that this chapter has helped you to think about the process of language development, and given you some practical ideas to help your child make more sense of people, and the things they say and do.

8

MOVING TOWARDS SPOKEN LANGUAGE

INTRODUCTION

When a child says his first word, it feels like a significant event to be celebrated and remembered. But this moment is actually one step in a long and complex process of learning language, involving much more than just speaking. As we've seen, children are usually very good at communicating, with body language and sounds, long before they say their first recognizable word. This process is less predictable for a child with autism, who is not fluent in those conversation skills – 'the pragmatics' – that in ordinary children come *before* speech. Whether or not your child has started to speak, he is likely to need extra help with expressing himself.

Please do read some of the other chapters in this book before continuing with this one, especially *Interactive Play*, *Teaching Pointing* and *Understanding Language.* Those ideas can help you to help your child build up the basic communication skills he needs, in order to move on to using spoken language himself.

This chapter is intended to give you more insight into this process, to help you clarify exactly how your child is expressing himself now, and to give you some ideas for how you might help him along. It includes looking at how your child might use gestures or more formal signs, and pictures or symbols, as well as speech. These other means of communication are used to *help* language development, sometimes enabling the child to remember and say words, and so acting as a 'bridge' to spoken language. However, some children with autism will need to rely on signs and symbols in the long term, as they continue to find learning to speak a difficult or even impossible task.

WHY DOES YOUR CHILD NEED OR WANT TO COMMUNICATE?

One of the first things to think about is what *motivates* your child to try to talk to you. The fact that *you* are very keen for him to speak is probably not important to him: pleasing an adult is not usually very motivating for a young child with autism! It may help to look at some of the reasons toddlers generally have for communicating, with some examples.

Some reasons why any young child might communicate

To *request*:

He needs help with basic physical comfort: he's hot or cold, hungry or thirsty, or has wet clothes.

He wants a particular food, drink, object or toy.

He wants you to do something; maybe to read a book or sing a song, to swing, chase or tickle him, or to put him in the bath.

He needs help with a task such as getting his clothes on or off, working the DVD player, opening or fixing something.

He wants *more* of something; food, drink or a game you've been playing.

To *refuse*:

He *doesn't* want what you are offering or giving him.

He wants you to *stop* singing, playing with or tickling him.

He doesn't want to do what *you* want him to do; maybe to wear a certain T-shirt, have a bath, put a puzzle away, or go into a particular shop.

To *find out*:

What something's called or what it is he can hear: 'Wassat?'

Where he's left a favourite toy: 'Where teddy?'

Where a certain person is: 'Granny?'

What's happening: 'Go car?'

To *share* – he wants you to:

See what he's noticed, and to respond when he points or comments.

Watch, join or clap him as he does a 'dance' or action or sings a song.

Share a smile, a cuddle or a lively game, so you know how he's feeling.

Know he's hurt himself or something has happened.

Have a 'chat' at his level: an exchange of movements, facial expressions, sounds or words.

All of these last five are particularly difficult for a child with autism, who needs the kind of *help in wanting to share* that we talked about in the chapter on *Interactive Play*.

HOW IS YOUR CHILD COMMUNICATING NOW?

Children with autism find it particularly hard to learn how to use both *body language* (facial expressions, eye-contact and gestures), and *spoken language*. Most children will find some way of letting you know what is most important to them, though they *may not be aware* that you want to know.

Parents are often, understandably, very keen for their child to begin speaking, and may get very focused on this. They sometimes think their child has *no* communication if he is not using any words. It is important to look at what your child *is* doing to communicate.

He might cry, throw himself to the ground, or push or pull you to a cupboard. It may take a lot of hard work on your part to find out exactly what he wants, and he may give up quickly: but these are all ways of communicating, and if you recognize them as such, you will have a starting-point for helping him move on.

You may have noticed that your child has started to let you know what he wants and doesn't want, in his own way. Your speech and language therapist might already have done some assessment, by observing your child closely and asking you some detailed questions about his everyday life. As we saw in the chapter on *Understanding Language*, formal testing is often not useful for young children with autism. It is more helpful in the early stages to watch, listen and take note of how he lets you know things, or whether you still have to guess.

How do you know he wants a favourite toy that's out of reach?

First, if your child never needs to let people know that he wants anything, because his favourite toys (and food) are always available, you may need to think about creating more opportunities for him to communicate (see below).

Here are some ways in which a child who is not yet speaking might show that he wants something he can see but not reach. These examples illustrate just a few of the many ways children communicate before speech: each shows a particular stage of awareness and skill in communication.

Stage 1: Pre-intentional

A child at the *pre-intentional stage* needs you to *interpret his behaviour*: he doesn't actively try or intend to communicate with you. For instance:

He goes and stands by the cupboard or shelf, and waits.

He goes and stands there and cries, looking up at or reaching for the object, but not looking at you.

He tries to climb up the shelves to get it.

Stage 2: Intentional but physical

The *intentional but physical stage* is often seen in young children with autism: they know that an adult can help, but don't know how to 'ask' you in a social way. For instance:

He tugs at your arm and pulls you over to the shelf, or pushes you from behind.

He climbs on to your back and tries to steer you towards the shelf.

He tries to 'throw' your hand up to the object.

Stage 3: Intentional social

These examples of *intentional social communication* are actually quite sophisticated methods of requesting, as they involve coordinating looking and eye-contact, with reaching or pointing and vocalizing. Many looking young children with autism will need to be taught

how to go through these stages, and then to move on to using some words or signs (see also *Teaching Pointing*).

He reaches up and vocalizes, looking back towards you for your attention.

He makes eye-contact with you as he reaches, then looks towards the object, and back to you.

He points to the object, makes eye-contact, and looks back to where he is pointing, making urgent vocal sounds all the time.

How does he ask for something that he *can't* see?

When the thing he wants is out of sight, or is not an actual object but an action, your child will have to go to further lengths to get his message across, and you may have to work harder to interpret the message. Children with autism do *not* usually invent gestures or act things out, to show you what they want: they often find this kind of body language just as hard as speech.

- In this situation, a young child who is still *pre-intentional* may just cry or get really frustrated, as he has no way of letting you know what he wants.
- Some *physical* methods of communication may still work. For example, your child may 'back up' to you to be picked up or swung round, or put your hand on his tummy for a tickle. He may seem to use your hand as a 'tool' to open a door or cupboard, or to get you to fix something.
- He may bring you an *object* to show you what he wants: perhaps your keys when he wants to go out, or an empty

chocolate wrapper when he is hungry. Maybe he just pushes this object at you, or maybe he makes eye-contact and vocal sounds as he brings it, using the object in a *social* way.

- He may find a *picture* such as a photo of Granny or a car when he wants to go out. He may just sit and hold the picture himself (*pre-intentional* communication), try to close your hand around it (*intentional physical* communication), or even point at it while trying to get your attention (*intentional social* communication with *gesture*).

Clearly, there are many different sorts of *non-verbal communication* or ways of communicating without speech. Some of these are really important even to people who can speak easily. We go on using facial expressions, gestures and other body language to illustrate, clarify and enliven what we are saying. When a young child with autism cannot make his needs known in more conventional ways, his familiar adults need to recognize and respect what he *is* doing, to help him experience successful communication and move on towards spoken language.

The list that follows shows some examples of how young children communicate, some of which may be used both *pre-intentionally* and *intentionally*. For instance, screaming or crying may be a child's response to fear, and you may need to interpret what he is frightened of. On the other hand, he may have learned that the only way he can stop you from taking him somewhere he doesn't like is to scream very loudly, so he does this on purpose to communicate that he doesn't want to go any further. It is sometimes hard to know which stage your child is at: you may have to watch and think carefully to decide.

Some ways that young children communicate	*Examples*
Body movement or position	Backing towards you to be lifted up Waiting by a door, shelf, cupboard etc. Lying down and going'stiff' or 'floppy' Backing off or hiding away
Physical	Putting your hand on something, or trying to 'throw' it towards a shelf Pushing or pulling you to something Climbing up behind you for a piggy-back Throwing things away or at someone
Gesture	Touch-pointing (picture in a book) Distance-pointing, to ask for or show something Putting arms up to be picked up Waving 'bye bye' Shaking or nodding head

Facial expression	Smiling or frowning Shutting mouth very tight Looking confused Going blank or 'tuning out'

Using objects	Bringing you a plate or food wrapper Fetching pyjamas when tired
Pictures	Bringing a photo of someone Choosing a book by the picture on the cover

Some ways that young children communicate	*Examples*
Vocal sounds	Squealing or screaming Crying, laughing, giggling Humming, singing, shouting Grunting or groaning Babbling, 'playing' with speech sounds
'Symbolic' sounds	Animal sounds; wind or rain noises Vehicle and machine noises
Spoken words	Unclear but recognizable in context Clear words or parts of words Echoed words or phrases Joined words or actual sentences

All of these examples can be effective, and we can encourage children who find using speech difficult to *use whatever ways work* to get their message across. As we've seen, children who are starting to use more *social* communication may combine several of these, such as pointing with vocalization and eye-contact. *Any* successful communication helps to keep a child motivated.

You may by now be ready to summarize *what* your child lets you know and *how* he does it in different situations. Just to help you get started, here's a way you might write this down, and how Adam's parents filled it in:

WHAT is he communicating?	*HOW does he communicate?*
He wants to watch his DVD	Brings the DVD and pulls me to the DVD player
He wants his blanket	Screws up his eyes and sucks his thumb
He wants a drink	Pushes his cup into my hand, and may echo – 'You want a drink'
He doesn't want what I am offering	Turns his head away or pushes my hand
He wants me to swing him round	Backs up to me, lifting his arms, and may hum our swinging song
He wants to play 'This little piggy'	Takes his sock off and gives me his foot. Sometimes takes my hand to his toes and makes eye-contact

Some ways that young children communicate	*Examples*
He wants to go outside	Stands by the door, may try to put on shoes
He wants to go into a particular shop	Stops outside, won't walk past
He has hurt himself or feels ill	Comes to sit with me quietly for a cuddle
He has seen a train (real or in a book)	Makes a train-like noise

As you fill in a 'How does he communicate?' column for yourself, you will probably notice that your child uses a *range of different ways* of communicating. The child in the example is using mainly body movement and position, with some objects, and occasional eye-contact, hummed tunes and symbolic noise. He sometimes echoes speech, but does not yet use spoken words spontaneously to communicate. At times his parents are not sure whether he has communicated intentionally or not: they still have to interpret some of his actions and sounds.

HOW YOU CAN HELP YOUR CHILD TO COMMUNICATE

Learning to communicate is closely linked to the development of play, social relationships and understanding language. The ideas suggested in other chapters in this book may naturally lead your child to be more interested in communicating and even to saying his first words. After some general ideas for making sure your child has the chance to use his skills to the full, we'll explain more about how your child might begin by using pictures or symbols, and gestures or signs. After that we'll concentrate on encouraging vocalization and speech.

Giving your child more opportunities to communicate

Whatever means of communication your child is using at the moment, you may need to accept and work with it for a while, at least until he is ready and able to move on and share what you are trying to teach him. The following suggestions apply to children at all the different stages.

- Do give him the benefit of the doubt: *respond to him as if he has communicated*, even if you are not sure he did so intentionally. Adam in his parents' summary above makes a train sound after seeing a train, which may just be his reaction to it. If someone responds with 'Yes, a train! Ch-ch-ch!' *as if* he was commenting and trying to draw their attention to it, he will have started a 'conversation' without even meaning to! He then has the opportunity to repeat the sound, this time intentionally.

- You need to make sure he has *time and space* to communicate. Make a short 'special time' to play with him regularly without distractions; make sure older brothers and sisters don't always speak *for* him; and *pause* during familiar activities, games and songs so that he can get one step ahead of you, and take an active part.

- Let him try to *express his needs for himself,* even if you know exactly what he wants. You could leave some favourite toys or food in sight but out of reach, or leave his pudding in the fridge after dinner and see if, and how, he lets you know that he wants it. You could also set up a situation where you 'forget' something vital, not to test or annoy him, but to help him find a way of requesting successfully. For example you give him paper without a pencil, a yoghurt without a spoon, or only one shoe.

- It is important to offer some *real choices* even if you think you know what your child wants: he may surprise you! Even if he makes the choice you expect between two toys or drinks that you hold out, he will have communicated positively. In a favourite active game such as 'Here we go…*up*!' you can introduce an alternative such as '…*round*!' then let him indicate which he wants by pausing after 'Here we go…'

- Make sure that your child has plenty of chances to *communicate spontaneously*, rather than becoming dependent on you to prompt or cue him in. It may be hard to hold back and wait for him to take the initiative, but you will be doing him a big favour. He must learn to feel the need for something and act on this feeling: you can't always be there to prompt him!

COMMUNICATING WITHOUT SPEECH

Some children with autism take much longer than others to start speaking, and (as we explained in *Teaching Pointing*), some with especially severe difficulties will not manage to speak, however hard

we and they try. This doesn't mean we should give up on helping them to express themselves better, even without spoken words. We know that using objects, signs and symbols can *stimulate* speech development for some children, as well as being an actual *alternative* when needed. Pointing, of course, can be very powerful and can do both these things. However, there comes a stage when pointing is not quite enough.

For example, how can he let you know about something that isn't in the room, or tell you that he wants an action or event (like carrying his trike into the garden, or a trip to the park)? We have already seen that some children use physical ways of communicating, or will bring objects such as their coat or your keys. Just as we can help him to understand us by showing him 'objects of reference' (see *Understanding Language*), we can help *him* make *us* understand by collecting objects that are associated with what *he* might want to tell us, and teaching him to use them himself. They are a bit limited as a method, since the collection could soon became unwieldy. However, they can be very helpful in moving some children on towards using signs and symbols for themselves.

As we saw in *Understanding Language*, and *The Beginnings of Structure*, objects, symbols and signs can all be used as 'visual clues' to help a child to *see what you mean* and so understand what *you* are saying. Once they are familiar to your child, he may also be able to *use* them to let you know what *he* wants – so they can all help him to express himself. Symbols and signs are very useful for some children as a way of communicating in the longer term; so we'll now look in more detail at how you might start introducing them.

Pictures and symbols

Your child may have learned to point to something he can see, and choose from two alternatives, but perhaps he has not yet found a way of letting you know about something that is not in view. Or maybe he's using physical communication when pointing isn't enough; dragging or pushing you to the kitchen or the front door. Now that he is attempting to express himself in this way it can be worth trying *symbols* in this situation. These are standard black and white line-drawings (for example the symbols illustrated in the *Beginnings of Structure* chapter), but you can substitute other pictures such as photographs or your own drawings if this is easier.

You will probably need to teach him what each picture or symbol means first, before he will be able to use them himself. For example, when he points to the orange juice for a drink, you *show* him the 'drink' symbol at the same time. (If he does find pictures useful, you can introduce more varied ones such as 'milk' and 'orange' at a later stage – don't introduce too many to start with.) He needs to learn that the symbol is associated with the drink, without you keeping him waiting, or insisting. Then, if you leave them easily available, one day he may *bring* the card to you or *point* to it, to ask for his drink.

There is also a more formal approach to using symbols that is now widely used: the Picture Exchange Communication System (PECS),[1] where children are systematically taught to 'exchange' pictures or symbols with an adult for things that they want. They gradually build up a repertoire of symbols for their favourite objects, toys and food, and keep these in a small folder. The emphasis is on helping them to use the symbols spontaneously when they want something, rather than always in response to being asked what they want by an adult. They later learn to use symbols to make sentences and express more complex ideas.

If you've read the chapter on the *Beginnings of Structure,* you may already be using pictures or symbols to help your child understand *what is going to happen,* perhaps showing him a photo of the bath as you say 'It's *bath*-time', or two symbols in sequence as you explain, 'First *shopping,* then *swings*'. If so, he will already be familiar with them, and may be starting to see that they could be useful to him. He might even push the swings card into your hand, to let you know what *he'd* rather do first!

If your child does find pictures or symbols useful to express himself, you will need to find a way of organizing them as the collection grows. Many people find it helpful to keep them in a transparent folder or photo wallet, or attached to a felt board with Velcro®. You could make a little 'swatch' by punching holes in the corners and threading them on to a ring; but they do need to be easily removable, so you can show two in sequence if necessary, or even take one away (perhaps when you have run out of cake or don't want him to have any more!). It is important that they are kept handy, both for you to use as visual clues, and for him to show you what he wants.

Gestures and signs

The signs most widely used with children with communication difficulties are taken from the Makaton vocabulary, and many are like exaggerated versions of the gestures we use naturally, such as 'come here', 'drink' and 'sit down'. They are not used as a '*sign language*', but simply to *clarify and emphasize key words in spoken language.* As well as helping a child to see what you mean (in a similar way to pictures and symbols), signs can be a very useful means of communication. Children who are able to imitate them can learn to use them instead of a word they can't say, or to 'cue themselves' in to remember and say the word.

As autism affects *all* forms of communication, your child probably won't automatically make sense of and use signs straight away. But if you can use some of them consistently as you speak, they may help him to understand, learn, remember and *use words.*

We wouldn't suggest deliberately setting out to teach a very young child to use signs, especially if he can't yet point. Even if he is good at imitating them, a young child with autism will still need help to *use them communicatively.* Remember that teaching him to point was not simply a case of helping him make the pointing shape with his hand! However, once they've learned to use pointing as a means of communication, some children do naturally move on to copy some of the signs they see being made to them. If your child starts to attempt some signs, you might try to use them more deliberately when you talk about his favourite things. He is more likely to be motivated to use the signs for things he likes such as 'apple', 'bath', 'train', 'car' and so on, rather than abstract words like 'please' and 'thank you'.

Sometimes when a child begins to use signs, especially if we are a little too keen for him to start, he will use one sign as a 'catch-all'. For example, he may use the 'apple' sign whenever he wants *anything*, rather than discriminating between different foods or toys. This probably means that he isn't really ready to use signs and words, as he hasn't realized that they are linked to and 'label' different things. In this situation it is better to continue with pointing, and maybe to try pictures and symbols, to help him ask for particular things and learn their names.

When a child with autism starts to use signs successfully to communicate, the actions and movements he makes may still be rather imprecise and difficult to 'read', especially for people who don't see him every day. Without pressurizing him, you can help him to make the signs more accurately. It is usually best to mould his hands gently into the right position rather than just expecting him to copy what you are doing. Sometimes it helps to stand behind him briefly to do this, or even in front of a mirror; but you need to make sure this doesn't interfere too much with the most important thing, which is the actual message your child is giving you.

Many parents worry about using signs and symbols, especially if their child has started to use some words, because they think it will discourage him from speaking. Somebody may even tell you it will make him lazy – it won't! In fact, research on these different 'augmentative communication systems' has shown the *opposite* to be true: they usually *help* speech rather than hinder its development. Remember that you always use signs *with* speech, not instead of it, so they can act as a bridge to spoken language. Children find them useful at different stages, and for varying lengths of time.

VOCAL AND SPEECH SOUNDS LEADING TO WORDS

The other chapters have described ways to encourage your child's first steps in communication. He may already be starting to use some words and phrases, or may need extra encouragement to take these steps. He needs to realize that using more sounds, and later words, is worthwhile and can be enjoyable as well as useful to him. The following ideas are quite general: your speech and language therapist will be able to give you some more specific advice for your own child.

Encouraging him to explore and play with mouth shapes and vocal sounds

Some children with autism are described as having been 'very quiet' as babies. Many miss out the stage of babbling, which is how babies practise lots of vowels and consonants, before they use actual words.

- *Repeat* and extend any mouth movements and sounds your child makes to encourage him to play more with his voice. At first, this may only interest him if you copy *exactly* what he does; soon, you can add to this copying with your own version of his sounds. Some children respond best if you really exaggerate your facial expressions and vowel sounds. You could add more of a 'sing-song' or dramatic voice, or even some home-made percussion if it helps to make it more enjoyable.

- You can sometimes take advantage of moments in front of a mirror, to copy faces and sounds, maybe adding face paints to hold your child's interest (but don't insist if he doesn't like it).

- You may be able to build up repetitive sound-play games together, using the sounds he already makes. Try repeating his sounds several times, or put two different ones together to make little patterns; or add an 'answering' sound to his. You might begin to sound a bit like babies babbling! Over time, you can gradually add more different sounds to play with.

- Some children are fascinated when you use 'their' sounds instead of the actual words in a favourite tune. So you might sing 'Twinkle Twinkle Little Star' to 'la', to 'bee' or even to 'ow', and your child may be tempted to join in.

- You could explore other things that might make vocalizing more interesting, such as making sounds into a microphone, kazoo, cardboard or plastic tube, saucepan, or tape recorder.
- If you respond to his sounds with interest, your child may eventually start to imitate some of yours. You might be able to keep a little 'conversation' of sounds going, even if it seems one-sided at first. Every so often, you can try slipping in a different speech sound, animal or mechanical sound, or other funny noise to the game, and see if he is ready for a bit more 'give-and-take'.

Encouraging him to start using words

Your child might have started to repeat or echo some sounds and words he hears you say, or he might still just be making his own favourite sounds. We'll look now at how you might help him move on to using single words. We are not suggesting that you 'teach' him directly to say words, but that you give him every opportunity to hear, understand and *start to use them in ways that mean something to him.* Just repeating a word in imitation is not really intentional communication; we want him to *say the word on purpose* to get a message across to someone else. *Meaning* is essential, just as it was in teaching pointing and signs.

Here are a few ideas for encouraging your child's first meaningful words.

Your own language is important

First, do remember that the way you speak to your child has a big impact on his language development (see the chapter on *Understanding Language*). Even if you think he understands a lot of what you say, he probably still needs to hear plenty of repeated words and simple short phrases, if he is to start using words himself. As you go about your everyday activities and play with him, you can (and probably already do) naturally emphasize and repeat key words in short sentences, especially those to do with things he is interested in.

For example:

> Hat. Here's your hat. Hat on! On your head.
>
> Look! A dog. Woof! It's a dog. Dog – woof woof – dog barking!

Build on the sounds he makes

Do help your child to 'turn sounds into words', even if you are not quite sure what you heard. If you respond positively and interpret his sounds *as if* they are meaningful words, he might be encouraged to say them on purpose later on.

For example:

> Katy is sitting in her high chair, watching her mum prepare her dinner. She makes a few sounds to herself quietly, 'ee, 'b-b-b', and her mum looks over to her and copies some of them. They have a little 'conversation' of repetitive sounds.

Katy makes a different sound, 'mm'. Her mum says, 'Mmmm, mmmm, yum yum' and they repeat this little exchange. Then Katy goes back to saying 'ee'. Her mum gives her a little piece of the cheese she is slicing and says, 'Cheese. Yes, cheese. Yum yum, cheese.' Katy says 'ee' again, and her mum says, 'Yes, *cheese*' giving her another piece. The conversation continues as Katy eats her dinner.

Tom loves being lifted high up in the air, in a repetitive play routine. His dad chants, 'Here we go UP!…' as he lifts him playfully upwards, then '…and DOWN' as he bounces him back on the sofa. If his dad pauses before

> repeating the game, Tom wriggles his body upwards and looks at his face to show that he wants to go up again.
>
> One day during this game, his dad notices that Tom makes a sort of grunting sound as he catches his breath on the bounce down – 'uh'. Dad waits for him to do it again, and says, 'Up? Tom says *up*!' and then a loud 'UP!' as he lifts him again.
>
> After a few repetitions, Tom is saying 'uh' almost every time, on purpose, and his dad is now waiting for it; if it doesn't come, he asks 'up?', and waits a moment longer before saying 'UP' and lifting Tom. Tom experiences the power of words to make his dad do something exciting.

Notice that in these examples, the adults don't stop to wonder, 'Was that a word? No, probably not' and don't make a big deal of it by saying 'Oh good girl, clever girl, you said cheese. Say cheese, again, CHEESE!', which can be very off-putting for a child with autism. They also don't worry that the words are unclear or have sounds missing at this stage. Instead, they respond immediately to the *meaning* of what *might have been* said, so the child is rewarded in a way that helps him or her to *see the point* of making those sounds, and begins to attempt words.

Offer him choices

Your child may find it very confusing to be offered a choice of two things, and sometimes it seems easier just to give him what you know is his favourite drink, toy, colour and so on. But as we saw in the chapter on *Teaching Pointing*, choices are really important: they give your child extra opportunities to communicate, and a sense of being able to *negotiate* with you. You may well find that any tantrums decrease too.

Objects, pictures, signs and words can be used to offer choices of two things (and later more than two), depending on the situation and what motivates your child. If you started offering choices while he was learning to point, you will be used to holding out two things, and asking, 'toast or bread?', 'puzzle or cars?' or whatever, and this may already have led to his attempts at saying words. You may also be used to giving choices within his favourite play routines and flexible action songs, as we described in the chapter on *Interactive Play*.

You can give your child choices in lots of everyday activities. Even when you are out with him, you can show him and ask, for example,

> *'This way or that way?' 'Swing or see-saw?' 'Chocolate or jelly beans?'*

As well as involving your child in decisions and giving him opportunities to communicate, this is a good way of helping him to learn and say some new and different words – to expand his vocabulary.

Help him to learn new vocabulary

It's worth taking an active part in deciding which words might be *helpful to your child*, in discussion with other people working with him. This means thinking about what is interesting and useful to *him*, as well as what *you* want him to learn.

You might decide to concentrate for a while on a particular group of words, such as body parts, favourite foods, people's names, animals, actions or vehicles, together with words that crop up naturally in everyday activities like 'more', 'down', 'stop', 'go', 'finished' or 'help'. You can then think of songs and rhymes, use pictures, books and real-life situations, and make up lots of simple games with and without toys, to help him to learn and use the new words. You will find more ideas in the *Sharing Conceptual Play* chapter.

Leave 'gaps' in songs, games and everyday activities

Pausing within the familiar songs and play routines of interactive play is often a really successful and enjoyable way to encourage your child to communicate. At first you responded to *any* look, smile or small movement, as if it was a contribution. Your child might naturally have started putting sounds or words into his favourite games and songs. If not, you could try *waiting just a little longer at key points*, to see if he is ready to move on to attempting words: for instance,

Old MacDonald had a farm, ee I ee I o,

And on that farm he had a…?

Try not to cue him in every time

Make sure that your child doesn't rely totally on your cues. Does he *wait* for you to say, 'What do you want?' or 'drink, say drink'? Young children with autism often get into this habit and become 'prompt-dependent', which means they can only communicate in response to what you say. If you know he can say the word, try to give him the *time and space to speak first* when he wants something.

For example, you could have some raisins nearby, or stop at the *end* of a short play routine or song, and just wait a few seconds *without* prompting or helping. You might have to wait a little longer than feels natural, to give him time to communicate spontaneously, but it's worth it. If he really can't request without your prompt, then do help him to get what he wants, but try again soon.

Help him to generalize

When he is using several single words, make sure that he can use them in *a range of different situations.* For example, if he only ever asks for a drink in the kitchen when he can see his own cup, you could show him over time that he can ask in other places, or when the cup is different or not visible, and even when someone else is looking after him. Or if he uses the word 'pull' only in the 'Wind the Bobbin' song, you could look for other opportunities to use the word yourself (for instance, getting boots off). Try making up games that include the word 'pull', such as a 'tug-of war' with a piece of soft fabric, or towing each other in a cart or box.

COPING WITH ECHOING

Some children with autism go through an extended period of echoing adults' speech. Of course, copying words and sentences is an important skill in learning to speak, and ordinary toddlers go through a phase of repeating words or phrases. However, children with autism often do it more automatically and carry on longer; they need extra help to find more creative and spontaneous ways of using words. Children who echo a lot often say more than they can understand. They actually say things that they don't fully understand themselves. Echoing is one part of the *inflexibility and repetitiveness* of autism. Even so, don't forget that it can be a real bridge to creative speech, and gives the child good practice in forming words and phrases.

If your child echoes a question you have just asked instead of answering it, this might mean that he hasn't understood what you asked. It could also be that he realizes he is supposed to answer a question but he doesn't know what to say.

What might help?

- Find a way of *showing* him what you mean, by pointing, or showing objects, pictures or symbols.
- Teach him how to answer some common important questions (like 'what's your name?' or 'where do you live?') by *modelling what to say.*
- Try to ask *fewer questions* for a while.
- You can also *make use* of your child's echoing. For example, use simple words and phrases, including his name, *to comment* on his play or what he's looking at, instead of lots of questions and instructions; then if he echoes he will be using appropriate language himself.
- Later on it may help to *teach him to answer 'yes' or 'no'* to straightforward questions. The signs for 'yes' and 'no' might help as reminders or cues. Children with autism do seem to have special difficulty with 'yes'; one way to help is to offer him a series of things you know he'll want, cueing the answer yes: 'Do you want a drink, y…?', 'Do you want your twiddler, y…?'. He partly echoes your cue for yes, but finds it works.

He may remember echoed questions and sentences and come out with them the next time he's in a similar situation. For example, he might say 'What do you want?' or 'Do you want a drink?' instead of 'I want a drink', or just 'drink'. Or he might repeat something you said to someone else a few days ago, such as 'I expect he's hungry, and needs a bath' – the link being that you are unlocking the front door.

This could be his best attempt at intentional communication at this stage.

What might help?

- Assume that he is attempting to communicate, and try to respond to his needs.
- Try to work out what he wants to say, and say it for him to copy.

Many young children with autism also remember and repeat jingles, songs or phrases from films, stories, DVDs and advertisements. They may simply enjoy doing this, or just do it automatically when they see or hear something that 'triggers' it. Some do it when they feel confused or overwhelmed, repeating familiar words can be a way of 'retreating' to feel safe. They may also come out with jingles or familiar phrases in situations where attention is on them, but they don't know what to say or do.

What might help?

- Try to work out whether your child is trying to communicate something, or whether he seems to be doing it just to 'take a break' (which perhaps he needs).
- See if you can join in and share the story or jingle (though he may not let you); or have a simple conversation about the book or DVD.

- Bring his attention back to something else you really need him to do or listen to.
- You may want to think carefully about the amount of time you let him watch DVDs, especially if he does this so much that he seems to be blocking out opportunities for communicating.

HELPING HIM TO PUT WORDS TOGETHER

As we have seen, many children with autism tend to copy whole 'chunks' of language. They may find these learned phrases and sentences very useful and effective in certain situations. But it's a bit like trying to learn a foreign language by heart from a phrasebook: you can say the sentences you've learned, but don't know how to put together new ones for different situations.

The things you've already been doing to help your child understand and use language may have naturally helped him to start making up his own little sentences. On the other hand, you might feel he is a bit 'stuck' with single words and learned phrases. He may need extra help to put words together *himself* to make new phrases and sentences. This is a really important stage, and your child may take some time to learn how to do it. Your speech and language therapist may give you some tailor-made ideas for your own child, but here are a couple of general strategies that can help.

Expand what he says

'Expanding' means *adding one word or idea* as you respond to what your child says. Make sure your voice sounds natural as you do this, and don't worry about the little words like 'a' and 'the' which aren't emphasized. For example:

Your child says	*You might reply*
Car	Yes, car. *Tom's* car.
Duck	Oh yes, a duck! Duck *swimming.*
Drink	Want a drink? *Co-o-ld* drink.
More	More? More *juice*!
Hat	Hat on *Jamie*!
Tickle	Tickle? Tickle *Katy*!

The idea is to *let him hear and learn how you can add words on, not* to tell him to copy you, or try to 'make' him say more then and there.

Use a word he already says, as a 'pivot' or jumping-off place

You can comment to your child using a favourite word in lots of different ways, which will help him to do the same thing for himself. For example:

Daddy coming	Kiss Daddy
Daddy lie down	Hug Daddy
Daddy sad	Drink (for) Daddy
Daddy('s) shoes	John('s) Daddy

Daddy hide

or

Pop bubbles	Bubbles gone
Blow bubbles	Bubbles falling
Big bubbles	Bubbles up
More bubbles	Bubbles (in) eyes

SOME QUESTIONS OFTEN ASKED BY PARENTS

How can I stop him from 'losing' words, as he learns new ones?

Children who have needed a lot of help with learning to use words sometimes stop using some of the earlier ones as they increase their vocabulary. It may seem that they can only retain a certain *number* of words. If you remind your child of the old ones by repeating familiar games, activities or songs, you might find that he can still use them with this help. Remember, he may also need extra practice with generalizing – using the words he knows in different situations.

Some children *whisper* their words until they are absolutely sure of them; and occasionally children become quieter and quieter, and eventually stop speaking. Try not to show your anxiety by pressurizing him to speak; go back to interactive play instead, and try some of the 'listening' activities in the chapter on *Sharing Conceptual Play*.

If he starts to use some words, should we *stop* encouraging pointing and signs or symbols?

No, do still encourage mixed ways of communicating. People with naturally good language continue to use gesture and other body language, which makes their speech livelier as well as expressing things that are hard to put into words. And children who are finding language difficult may still need to use pointing, symbols or signs when the words they know aren't enough. Also they may want to combine two ideas before they know how to put words together. For example, one child would say 'bubbles' and point to where he wanted them to be blown, long before he could say 'Bubbles up there'.

How can I help him to play with other children?

Young children with autism often need so much support in the early stages of communicating, that at first they are only successful with adults who know them really well. Other children may think they *can't* play or are 'unfriendly', as they don't share the same way of communicating. Brothers, sisters and other children can be taught to understand and respond to a child's particular style, and can learn some of the games and songs that he plays with adults. A young child with autism will also need plenty of opportunities to play *alongside* others, and may need help to develop shared games gradually. Some can learn how to use specific sentences or 'scripts' to get started. For instance, we might teach a child to say 'Chase me' and run away, looking back over his shoulder, or to say 'Can I play?' when he's interested in someone else's game, like the child in the picture at the beginning of this chapter.

FINALLY

Children start to speak when and if they are ready and motivated to do it. You can't *make* your child speak, but we have suggested lots of ways to help and encourage him. It is important to try to see things from his point of view, and to use whatever motivates him and helps him to learn. We want him to see the *point of communicating*, and enjoy it, as well as to get better at expressing his needs and interests.

Learning language is a long and complex process, and is harder for some children than for others. It depends on learning many different skills, and on having those all-important opportunities to use them. It is really more amazing that anyone ever gets it all sorted out, than that some children find it difficult!

NOTE

1. Further information about PECS can be found at www.pecs.org.uk.

9 SHARING CONCEPTUAL PLAY

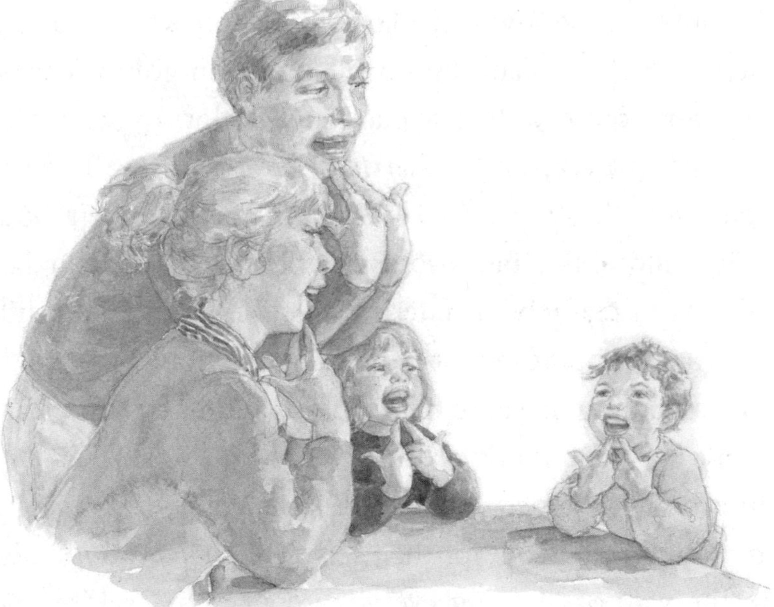

INTRODUCTION

This is the second chapter about play in this book. The first one, *Interactive Play*, should be read before this one because it gives you ideas for helping a child with autism to find his way into the social world as early as possible – even if you have only just begun to suspect that autism is his problem. Play that highlights the pleasure of sharing the fun with another person, or doing things *in turn* with someone so that you are both aware of the 'together' feeling, gets any child ready for the next stage in communication: real intentional dialogue or conversation, whether in gestures or in words as well. This is why simple interactive play takes priority.

As it becomes easier to engage and interest your child socially, though, you will probably begin to feel that you want more from his play, and that you would like to build on what you've already achieved in having made him a bit more outgoing. Perhaps you already know quite well that play and exploring are a really important part of every child's *development of thinking*. Through play, children learn things that will develop not just their bodily coordination and skills, but also their thoughts and their language. And you may already be wondering whether your child's difficulties with language will mean that he needs extra help with his thinking and understanding, because his thoughts might be less clear to him if he can't put them into words.

Children with autism are *not just hampered by their language problems* in finding things out for themselves; their *inflexibility* also often gets in the way of learning everyday concepts. Children who just watch the same two DVDs over and over give themselves little opportunity to compare different ones and make new preferences; children who line up their little cars and insist on them staying in the same order make it difficult to use them for any other kind of play. At a later stage, one child knew by heart the registration number of every car belonging to the three houses on each side of his own house, but hadn't discovered that three sweets and two sweets made five sweets; another could name 20 types of bird from pictures in her favourite information book, but wouldn't recognize a real robin if she saw it on the lawn outside. Once the channels of interaction open up, though, the child has opportunities to learn from the people around him, and interactive play itself can become more complex.

Some children are quite anxious and inward-looking, perhaps because they have such difficulty in making sense of what they see and hear that they are overwhelmed by fear of the unknown. Some may be hyperactive or 'flitting', especially in their pre-school years: they seem driven on by their own physical energy, and they are unable to stop, look and concentrate on one activity for more than a few seconds. And some get 'hooked' on very repetitive play with one object – swinging doors, spinning something, or looking at their fingers or a 'twiddler' from every angle.

Children with any disability will be far more dependent than other children on having an adult playmate and 'provider' of experiences, and for much longer. Without the attention, understanding, imagination and patience of an adult, most of their opportunities to learn and develop through play would never get going. Children with autism are different from other children with problems, though, in that they don't at first realize that adults could enrich their play; they tend to prefer solitary play, and would rather have *repetition* than enrichment. In our enthusiasm to help our child to learn, we mustn't forget the *voluntary and exploratory nature* of true play. We are not trying to drill our child into learning; we need to set up opportunities that will help him to find out that play *is* fun, and worth the extra effort that it takes for him. We *invite* the child to play, and we try to make it possible for him to accept our invitation.

In all this, our aim when we play with him is not only to help our child to *want* to learn new skills, but also to give him the feeling that he has some mastery and power over his experiences. This is an important part of *learning to be a person*, not just a helpless baby: something every child has to do. What he learns in his play in turn affects the way he copes with the 'real' world and 'real' life. *A growing child uses his play to make sense of the world around him.*

WHAT MIGHT GET IN THE WAY OF PLAY – AND WHAT MIGHT HELP?

We've already mentioned the *inflexibility and rigidity* of the way children with autism tend to think and behave; and this can come in many forms. Ordinary children may have their favourites among their toys, and carry around a shabby old teddy or dog-eared book wherever they go, but they also enjoy variety. They take pleasure in discovering variations on a familiar theme; when their parents join them in their play, they welcome their suggestions of new ways of playing with an old toy. A child with autism, though, often resists such changes; he seems to have his own rules for how a particular object should be played with, and (if he lets you join in at all) he may protest fiercely at your new ideas. As we talked about in the chapter on the *Beginnings of Structure*, we want to help him open his mind to a *range of possibilities* for particular toys or activities.

Another example of resisting change concerns the strong fascinations many children with autism have with certain types of object, so that other ideas don't get a look in. Sam's mother was asked whether Sam seemed to explore a new toy when he first started to play with it. She thought about that carefully, and said that he *looked* as if he was exploring it; then she added: 'But actually, I know he's just asking himself "Is there a lock or a key in here?" – and if there isn't, he's simply not interested'. Sam's fascination with locks and keys prevented him exploring anything else fully.

The trouble is that we really do want our children to think in an open-minded way, otherwise their intellectual growth is restricted, at least for the time being. Sam's way of exploring a toy was to ask himself a *closed* question: one that only had the answer 'yes' or 'no'. Ordinary children explore a toy by asking themselves open-ended questions: 'What sort of a thing is this?' – 'What does it do?' – 'How does it work?' – 'What else could I do with it?'; and these questions have the potential to carry the child's thoughts forward without restrictions, and even let him reconsider them as he gets more used to the toy.

Realizing the importance of a child's open-mindedness gives us a problem. We can't force our child against his will to play open-mindedly; play is supposed to be fun, pleasurable, self-chosen – in fact, playful. And yet we know it matters. So we must try to make it easier for him, and that means compromise.

The work you have already done on *Interactive Play* has been a good preparation, because it will have made your child more interested in you and what you do, and perhaps more inclined to share his play with you. Now you would like him to accept more of *your* ideas into his play. *Go very slowly at first* – don't expect to be able to change the things he is most single-minded about at this stage. For instance, if he is a child who lines things up and insists on them remaining in the same order, don't choose this as the first activity to change – respect the line that he has made, comment on it without touching it, and then perhaps start making your own line (or maybe a circle) a little way away, using components that are different from his. If he gets interested in your line, and wants to add to it (or start curving his own lines), he's already opening up his ideas a little, and you have helped him to do so on his own terms. It may help you to look at the section on '*Choosing priorities*' in the *Beginnings of Structure* chapter.

In the same way, if he plays with certain toys or objects very repetitively, don't insist that he shares this routine with you while you change some of his rules; try using similar materials as you sit a few

feet away, but use them just a bit differently, commenting on what you are doing: 'Mummy's making a big tower, UP it goes and... DOWN it falls'; 'Daddy makes the ambulance go NEE-NA, NEE-NA'. If it seems that you are having fun, but not pressurizing him to join in, you may find he is tempted to join you and try out new variations. If he has become used to turn-taking through interactive play, perhaps he'll take turns in trying out new ideas too.

Many parents say that their child begins to show a sense of humour through interactive play. Often this happens when the child sees you doing something familiar but in a slightly bizarre way, and realizes that *this* change might be funny, not threatening. In the chapter on *Moving Towards Spoken Language*, Jamie has a big grin on his face as his mother puts her best hat on his head; another pre-school child with autism made his first joke when he held his cup upside-down on his head, saying 'Cup-hat!' Both *changes* and the *concept of joking* are difficult for children with autism – and so is the idea of *pretending* (pretending a cup is a hat for instance) – but somehow the element of the bizarre and the humour of the moment helped this child to understand what pretending was about.

You might even be able to develop a game that is repetitious but also includes change and surprise *as part of the ritual* – remembering that ritual gives the child the structure he needs to feel safe. For instance, you could set out about eight or ten plastic mugs in a circle of varied colours, upside-down, and hide a different small plastic animal under each, randomly, so that your child can't easily predict what is under each mug; then let him turn each one up to see what is there, while you dramatically react in surprise. The point here is that each time you or he takes a turn of hiding the animals, they will be in different places because there are too many to match, and no system to match them by; and this will help him to be a little more flexible. (This doesn't stop you playing a matching game at another time, perhaps matching different colour bricks to different colour mugs, and using only three or four – that's a game with a different purpose.)

IMITATION

A more socially complex game involves imitation, but still allows your child to play with the ideas of change and jokiness within a safe ritual. Imitation is obviously an extremely useful skill, which all children need in order to learn a whole range of other skills, and of course to learn words and how to use them. Ordinary children imitate naturally from the first six months of life, and almost always their imitation is *social*: that is, you can see that they are *aware* that they are trying to do the same thing as you are doing, by the way they look at you, give you eye-contact, smile and try again. Children with autism have much more difficulty in imitating, and don't make a social game of it – they seem to imitate in a kind of social vacuum, and often even wait until you've turned away before they do it. And sometimes, as we saw in looking at *echoing* (*Moving Towards Spoken Language*), once imitation comes they do it very inflexibly.

All the same, *social* imitation is such an important skill that we must try to teach it; and to do this through play is the best chance we have. Remember the obvious fact that it is easier for *us* to imitate *him* than for *him* to imitate *us*; we talked about this in the *Interactive Play* chapter. At its simplest, we can start at this level and try to get a turn-taking sequence going with sounds. For example:

> Daniel happens to cough, and his mother copies the cough exactly.
>
> Daniel ignores her, but coughs again (he has a tickly throat).

> His mother copies him, this time with more emphasis.
>
> When he coughs again, she does it again loudly, and makes eye-contact if she can. Daniel's attention is caught, and he coughs again, this time almost experimentally. His mother replies with another cough, then says 'Daniel coughs – Mummy coughs!' and she repeats her cough. Daniel coughs again, and looks expectant. Now he is imitating as much as she is, and is doing it socially.

You can go on to try creating such sequences with any sound your child happens to make. Once he is beginning to imitate your sound, try introducing a new and intriguing sound that isn't so familiar to him – in the end you are hoping for a series of sounds where you imitate each other and either of you changes the sound every now and then, for as long as you are both finding it fun.

With luck you can make it more complex, using both sounds and actions together, and still remembering that he needs you to demonstrate the idea of social imitation by *you* imitating *him* to start with. Ordinary children love this game too, and it might help the child with autism to get the hang of it if brothers and sisters join the imitation as well; or parents might imitate the child together. Choose a moment when he spontaneously makes a sound *and* action (such as banging a spoon on the table and shouting 'der der der', or even jumping and squealing in excitement) and do the same thing for a moment, then stop and wait for him. (If more than one of you are imitating, this can be quite dramatic, and he may pause and look at you in astonishment.) Whatever he does next, imitate again, once more stopping and waiting for his turn. Continue as long as he enjoys it, but don't pressure him – you may need to wait for a more relaxed moment, and try again.

It helps to have a name or 'signal' for this game; one family calls it the 'D'dah!' game because their signal for the game to start is to announce 'D'dah!' dramatically with their hands above their heads. For a while it will be the child with autism who makes a series of actions and sounds for the others to imitate (which can be very satisfying for him, as you can see from the picture at the beginning of this chapter), but eventually one of the imitators can offer a simple but striking action or sound, and see if he will imitate them in his turn. And this is likely to be a much more flexible and social form of imitation than we usually expect in autism at this age, and it can be built on in increasingly complex ways. As always, we try to make the foundation and framework of a quality to support further progress; and in this game you are also increasing his powers of concentration (watching and listening), which again are essential to his learning.

CONCENTRATION

Sometimes it's suggested that one of the chief problems in autism is lack of concentration. We can't really agree with that, when we see children concentrating all too completely on the things that fascinate them – objects that spin (whether washing machines or spinning coins), TV aerials, reflections in metallic surfaces, swinging doors, darts or snooker programmes on television, and Thomas the Tank Engine, to name just a few typical favourites. It might be more true to say that they seem to concentrate on things that don't appear to lead them on anywhere, instead of the things that we would think interesting and fulfilling.

It really doesn't help to overencourage these fascinations, in the hope that eventually the child will get sick of them; he won't. However, at least we know what motivates him, and sometimes we can use this motivation as a 'way in' and then try to broaden his interest a little from that point. For instance, a child might be happy to help his mother make a Thomas the Tank Engine cake, and be led on from that in three different directions: playing at other kinds of cooking, getting interested in trains and transport generally, and trying other methods of making pictures of Thomas. In a way, *we* are trying to achieve *variation* within the 'category' of things that the child already likes.

If you've been successful in using interaction games with the old familiar rhymes in the ways described in *Interactive Play*, you may be able to move much more physically close to your child through these, sitting side by side on the sofa or taking him on your knee. Rhymes like 'This little piggy went to market', 'Round and Round the Garden', 'Patacake', 'Horsie, Horsie', 'Wind the Bobbin' and 'This Is the Way the Lady Rides' don't just give you the chance of a cuddle; they encourage him to watch and listen *to you* because both the words and the actions become so familiar, and remind the child of each other, keeping his attention going. Action rhymes also give the child a sense of *anticipation and sequence* – the 'I know what's coming next' feeling – and this helps him to feel as if he's in control, and encourages his ability to concentrate on a whole series of actions. Finger games (such as 'Incy Wincy Spider') take this further, helping both imitation and hand–eye coordination. If you've forgotten the words and actions, you'll find plenty of helpful illustrated books in the children's section of your local library or toy library.

You may still find that your child refuses to sit on a lap if it means looking at your face. If your child is like this, don't give up on lap play; turn your child with his back to you (either on your lap or on the couch beside you) and bring your hands round in front of him to do the actions. You could try sitting in front of a mirror.

In time he may tolerate facing you more closely in order to get a rhyme he has come to enjoy. Parents sometimes feel unhappy about seeming to *impose* a loving touch on a child who doesn't appear to like it; but don't ever give up on getting in a quick cuddle, or even just a passing hug or stroke. He *will* come to like it sooner or later if you gently persist, especially if he associates it with activities that he enjoys, and if you haven't made a struggle of it.

CHILDREN WHO HAVE LEARNING DIFFICULTIES AS WELL AS AUTISM

Ordinary children are led on in their play by the excitement of their own thoughts. They look at a toy or other unfamiliar object, and at once, as we've seen, all sorts of questions come into their minds: What's this for? What could I do with it? What will happen if I do *this* – or *that*? When they try out these questions, what does happen will suggest more ideas to them, and so their exploration becomes more and more complicated.

For a child who has learning difficulties as well as autism, the interesting questions don't so quickly come to mind, and they don't so easily lead on to further ideas. The child's activity with a toy may come to a full stop, because his thoughts have come to a full stop. At this point, instead of continuing to look at and explore the toy, he may drop it or throw it aside – CRASH! – and suddenly he finds he's done something interesting. This is one way a child with limited ideas may learn to throw toys as his *main* activity with them; and this in turn prevents him keeping the toy in his hands long enough to find out about more adventurous possibilities for play with it. We should also remember that many children with autism find the fast movement of something past their eyes particularly *visually* exciting.

When a child seems to have 'got stuck' in his play – as if he isn't aware of the next possibilities – you need to start thinking about what he finds rewarding *now*, and how you could build on that. If he repeatedly throws things, it's fine to say clearly 'Luke – no throwing!' but also make sure you show him a more positive way. By your close involvement, encourage him to build higher before knocking down the pile. Make him soft beanbags to *throw into a laundry basket* (so that throwing is transformed into the more positive skill of *aiming*); and try a sound-maker (bells, jam jar lids) in the basket, to encourage him to listen as well as throw. Perhaps there are particular kinds of sounds he enjoys? Show him new ways of producing similar sounds, help him to try out new sound-making activities, gradually increase the variety and introduce him to rhythm, encouraging him to use his body in time with the sound.

Parents of children with autism often feel that their child simply *does not* play. It is true that some children with autism may appear to have no desire to play or explore. It may help us to try to see this from the child's point of view. If we think of the child's behaviour as his attempt to make sense of his world – remembering that he may feel he has no control over it – we can then try to *think ourselves into his difficulties.* Do the noises that his toys make help him to understand them better – or do they frighten and confuse him? Are his toys full of unpleasant surprises? (Most children like surprises that they are half-expecting.) Would *you* be bored with this toy if you had his problem? – or perhaps find it too complicated to see the point of? Has he given up in despair because he is too 'flitting', and therefore can't concentrate long enough, to get to the toy's most exciting moment – its climax or 'pay-off'?

Thinking ourselves into the child's skin like this can often make us realize *why* he is not finding it pleasant to play. We are then

halfway to working out ideas for making play both possible and rewarding for him, and therefore a satisfying learning experience.

It's not always a matter of enlarging on a child's play. With some children, one gets the feeling that things are so confused and chaotic for them that what they most need is someone to make things calm and very simple. For a child like this, a quiet room and a patient adult who will lead him through the possibilities of *one toy at a time* are most helpful – a rich variety only confuses him all the more.

'A GROWING CHILD USES HIS PLAY TO MAKE SENSE OF THE WORLD AROUND HIM'

This is probably the most important sentence in this chapter so far, because it's our job to make play work in the same way for a child with autism as it does for other children. Play may not come naturally to him, but we can still find ways of making it happen and making it useful. If that makes it easier for him to make sense of the world around him, instead of feeling confused and anxious, then it must be worth a lot of effort from us.

When you come to think about it, the word 'sense' can be used in two rather different ways. We've used it here as 'meaning': *making sense of things* is the same as *getting meaning from them.* But we also talk about 'the five senses' – hearing, seeing, smelling, touching and tasting.

We use these five senses to get bits of information that we can then put together (using our brain) in order to *make sense* or *get meaning*. The bits of information on their own are not much use until we can make sense of them by working on them in this way. All the same, the more practice we get in *attending to* what our senses tell us, the better we shall be able to put our bits of information together in order to get at their meaning.

We can help a child with autism to attend to what his senses are telling him by the way we play with him; and we can also help him to learn about meaning by making sure there is a real meaning for him, and helping him to find it. We need to bear in mind, though, that there is actually another sense that we all take for granted in other children, even if they have poor sight or hearing: the sense of *social empathy*. Ordinary children naturally have *a sense of what it is like to be somebody else* – almost automatically, they 'put themselves in your shoes', and guess at what you might be thinking or feeling. Even when they can only just walk, they'll come and show you something that they find interesting, because they expect that you'll be interested too. That hotline to other people's feelings is *social empathy*, and it is very weak indeed in autism; but empathy is the vital ingredient for communicating fully in a social world – and extremely difficult to teach. A child with autism all the more needs our help to get the best information he can from the senses that are left to him, and to make it meaningful. With luck, empathy may improve.

Actually we might do better to use different words to describe the 'five senses'. Words like 'see' and 'hear' are a little bit passive, and in fact they remind us that most of us can't help seeing and hearing the sights and sounds that pour into our eyes and ears. But if we are going to concentrate on meaning, we should be trying to make our child an *actively sensing* person. That means that we must help him not just to hear, but to *listen*; not just see, but *look*; not merely touch, but *feel and explore*; not only smell, but *sniff to get the smell*; and not passively taste, but *actively savour*.

Let's think now about how we might make our child aware of all these possibilities for learning.

Helping your child to listen

Don't forget that listening *to people* is especially difficult for a child with autism, and likely to go on being so (in the school classroom, for instance). This is partly because the child tends *not to notice the body language* in somebody else which signals that they are about to speak, and so he's unprepared for it; and partly because parents and teachers often try to speak to a *group* of children together, but the child with autism doesn't count himself as belonging to that group. In helping the child to attend to what he hears, the fact that your voice is a part of that experience could prepare him better for school later on.

First, if you normally have 'wallpaper music' or TV on just for company (or to soothe your child), remember that this damps down other sounds and teaches him *not* to listen. Ration yourself!

We want him to realize:

- that there are *lots of different sounds*. Listen for different sounds yourself, and show him you're listening in an exaggerated, 'acting' way – fingers on lips, eyes open wide – to try to get him to listen too. Make sounds happen yourself, close to his ear if they're tiny sounds – rustling paper or cellophane®, phone dialling tone, ticking watch, ballpoint click – and get him to copy the sound himself in the same way. Have a really noisy session sometimes – banging saucepans, stamping feet, blowing mouth organs, turning up the CD player and singing as well. (But some children with autism find certain noises very stressful to hear – watch out for that, and stop quickly if he's showing stress.)
- that sounds can be *the same but different*. Play about with variations on the same sound: a voice can be high or low,

loud or soft, for instance – see if he can imitate you in '*whisper, whisper, whisper*', '*SHOUT, SHOUT, SHOUT!*' Or change from a tiny tapping noise to a loud banging noise. Xylophones give different notes, but it's just as much fun to try how a spoon sounds when tapped on ten different objects. One father strung up different sized empty tins for banging (make sure there are no sharp edges); bottles with different amounts of water in them are wonderful if you can be sure that your child won't break them. Try scratching or finger-flicking different surfaces. Let him stir, in three separate bowls, dried peas, rice and sugar, and notice the different sounds (when he can understand well enough, you can develop this into guessing games)

- that *voices can imitate other sounds*. Parents naturally imitate the sneezes and coughs of their small children – and it's good that they do, because this teaches the child to imitate in turn. We do it with other things too – for lots of children, 'brrmmm-brrmmm' is their first 'word' (though seldom for children with autism). Extend this deliberately – say 'bang' loudly when you hear one, imitate the washing machine, the cat or dog, a creaking door, the 'ssshh' of a fast-flowing tap and the gurgle of water going down the plughole – and encourage your child to do it too

- that *sounds have direction*. He needs to be able to locate sounds – try asking *him* (with exaggerated questioning looks) where everyday sounds (motorbike, ice-cream chimes, barking) are coming from. If he's beginning to understand jokes, look in all the unlikely places until he shows you. Make a game of shaking a toy behind him to one side – he gets the toy if he turns in the right direction.

Go and look for a heard sound together – cat, lawnmower, road-drill. With the help of one or two other people, you can make the game of listening for and finding a sound quite complicated

- that *sounds are meaningful*. Talk about and demonstrate what messages different sounds are conveying to you. When you hear clinking milk bottles, a car arriving, the doorbell, the baby crying, rain or wind, footsteps, letters on the mat, the phone – try to get him to listen with you first, then say what it is, then let him see you react to what it means (or let him react himself – fetch the letters, for instance). If he's reached the guessing-game stage, have three different noise-making things on the table (such as saucepan and lid, two spoons, two tins) and let him 'hide his eyes' and guess which made the noise – or let him make *you* guess.

Helping your child to look

We want him to realize:

- that *looking is interesting*. Make a collection of scraps that are exciting to look at – not just pictures, but interesting patterns, metallic paper with reflective surfaces, bits of glittery or shimmery material, feathers and so on – stick them in a cardboard book or plastic album, and make it a bit of a treat to go through them with him. Many children with autism are interested in reflections: show him that you are too – imitate your reflections in a mirror, seek out reflections in puddles and shop windows when you're out, jump on each other's shadows on a sunny day. Spend time looking out of the window with him, and try this song (to the tune of 'For He's a Jolly Good Fellow'):

> Looking out of the window, looking out of the window,
> Looking out of the wi-in-dow – to see what we can see!
> We can see a…[wait for him to choose, if he can]…TREE
> We can see a TREE
> A tree in the garden, a tree in the garden, a tree in the gar-ar-den –
> THAT'S what we can see!

Continue as long as he's interested; other members of the family may like to join in, and it's a good song for the car or train as well. You may remember this song from the *Interactive Play* chapter; here, it's a good example of how shared play can become more complex as your child develops both pointing and spoken words

- that *exploring by looking is worth his while.* Try to prevent him dropping or throwing a toy: he needs to look long enough to find what's interesting about this one. 'Talk him round' the toy, helping him to discover its most attractive features; in an action toy, make sure he's looking at the moment the action takes place. If there's some sort of climax or moment of success, emphasize it with your own exclamations of enthusiasm or praise – make him feel it was *his* success, even if it was mostly yours. That might make it worth his while to have another go, looking more carefully this time

- that he can *find what he wants by looking.* Don't just put a toy in his hands and leave it at that – encourage him to make a choice from two or three, so that he looks from one to another. While he's looking at a toy he likes, cover it with a cushion and encourage him to find it – help him by giving him a peep if necessary. Peep-bo and hide-and-seek games of all sorts will help him to look: remember that children with autism often find *scanning to find something* visually difficult. Use containers of many kinds – boxes with and without lids, paper bags, old handbags, a cloth bag with an elasticated opening – to put toys in for him to search for

- that *pictures represent objects.* Put pictures on walls where he can see them (and talk to him about them), but choose them carefully – they should be clear pictures of familiar things. Avoid cartoon-like drawings and fussy designs that are difficult to see – some alphabet or animal friezes and photo posters are especially good. The same with picture books: early on, look for simple card books that won't tear. Cut pictures from catalogues and magazines for a talk-about scrapbook. Make an object-to-picture matching game: find pictures of familiar objects (or use a digital camera if you've got one), stick them on cards, and match them as closely as you can with actual objects. We did this with a key, comb, clothes peg, toy car, plastic elephant, cotton-reel, pine cone, string of beads, pencil and spoon: show your child the picture, and let him find the object to put beside it (perhaps from a choice of only three to start with). Later you could make another set of pictures that don't look quite the same as your objects (a different kind of key or type of car, say), so that he has to match the *general concept,* not the exact appearance – which is more difficult

- that some things are *like each other,* some different. Look for toys that involve matching – colour to colour, shape to shape, size to size. In the kitchen, in the street or park, point out *same and different*: big spoon, little spoon; one red car and another red car just the same; here's a daisy, that's a buttercup, here's *another* buttercup. Match pictures together, either your own duplicate photos or ready-made from a game of 'snap' or picture-dominoes. Make him a little album with photos of the *people* he knows best, and talk about them while he looks: 'Jane and Amy have *both* got long hair – Ben's hair is short'.

Helping a child to touch and feel

We want him to realize:

- that things in the world have *many different characteristics* that he can discover by reaching out and touching. They can be hard, soft, cold, warm, wet, dry, furry, soggy, prickly, springy, powdery, hairy, smooth, rough, jagged, crumbly, holey, crackly, damp, long, short, heavy, light, wobbly, mobile, firm, thin, thick, big, little, tall, malleable, bumpy, sticky, alive, flexible, stiff, round, hollow, flat, top-heavy, hinged, twisted, many-sided, greasy, pourable, stirrable, silky, scratchy, spongy – and combinations of these. There are 50 'feely' words here, and if you think of an object to fit each of these words, you will already have a variety of touch experiences for your child – yet if you walk round your kitchen or into a garden, you will find many objects that aren't fully described by these words.

  A few children (sometimes described as 'tactile-defensive') hate certain touches. If your child is like this, don't *impose* these on him, but don't give up either. You may be able to improve his motivation, or find a pleasant

association (sound or visual). You could even keep a warm damp flannel or rough towel ready to 'wipe off' a sensation he doesn't like and increase his tolerance that way

- that *touch has meaning* – it tells us something about what can be done with an object. Round things roll, prickly and spiky things may hurt if we press them too hard, sticky things leave their stickiness on our hands, and so on. Later your child may learn about the *combinations of characteristics* that make some things float, some sink, some break, some fold, and other interesting qualities. As before, offer your child the experience, talk about it (even if he doesn't understand everything you say), demonstrate it

- that hand and finger touch gives better information if we *handle things delicately*. Some children have no midway between clutching and dropping. They have to learn to hold and turn things gently in their fingers if they are to use hand and eye together; they must hold in one hand and touch with the other to explore and use toys effectively. Sometimes this itself has to be taught, perhaps in a similar way to teaching pointing. Once your child has got the idea, try making a 'feely bag' to hide familiar small objects in – with a gap in each side seam for his two hands to enter: he finds the object you ask for by two-handed touch alone

- that there is *enjoyment to be got* from hand and finger touch. Some children love to finger and follow a raised pattern, to stroke their mother's hair or their father's beard, or to feel his stubbly chin. Some like to touch the softness of a sleeping baby's cheek or of a cat's delicate ears. Encourage this sensuous feeling – they are learning to touch gently, and to think about what they are touching

- that there is pleasure and excitement to be found in *whole-body touch experiences*. Such experiences might be: being snuggled and rough-handled in a warm towel after a bath; splashing in the bath or in a swimming pool (if he's scared of the slippery bath, put a small towel under him, or put a plastic clothes basket in the bath and let him sit in that); kicking about in a pile of dead leaves (do it together); walking in a high wind; trying to balance in deep mud; rolling down a grassy slope or on heather; bouncing on a trampoline or inflatable; riding a merry-go-round or a pony; swings, slides toboggans and see-saws. Some of these experiences can be frightening; if your child is nervous, don't insist on them (the point is that he should *enjoy them*!), but try to see what is scaring him and how you could reassure him and bring back the fun. These experiences give him valuable understandings about the qualities of the natural world; but they are also exciting, and the child begins to *share* his excitement with other people. They are therefore likely to encourage his social communication as well.

Helping your child to use his sense of smell

We want him to realize:

- that smells *have variety*. Comment on the different smells that you come across during the day, nice or less so! Use gestures as well, to show that you're noticing smells – hold or twitch your nose, make a 'really appreciative' face.

Remember that he may like smells that you don't, and vice versa: there's a lot of disagreement among different people about the smells of petrol, strong cheese, subway trains, tobacco – and lots of people like their own body smells even if they dislike other people's. So don't force smell preferences on him, even though you'll try to put him off dabbling in the toilet, or worse!

- that he can *sniff at smells voluntarily*. Most children get mixed up between sniffing and blowing – help him by finding him interesting things to sniff and by play-acting yourself. Offer him a variety of smells – creosoted wood, fragrant leaves bruised in your fingers, cinnamon, ginger and curry, sour milk, suede, vinegar. Obviously, don't actually let him play with things he might eat or spill, but don't let the necessary restrictions cut him off from these sensory experiences

- that *smells have meaning*. Often we identify a situation first by its smell – for instance, that the toast's burning,! Share these and other meanings with your child – 'The milk's gone sour', 'There's a bonfire somewhere', 'Dinner's nearly ready', 'Daddy's made coffee', 'Jane's painting her room'. Help him also to recognize the characteristic smells of common objects – orange, lemon, soap, cocoa, onion and so on. One mother made a 'box of smells' to interest her child – inside small muslin bags she sewed such 'smellies' as an old perfume bottle, cloves, a teabag, coal tar soap, dried orange peel and peppermint – some children would enjoy guessing at the smells, others would just like sniffing at them.

Having said all this – there are certainly some children with autism who are oversensitive to smells in a rather undiscriminating way. They may smell every bit of food and reject a lot of it, or they may embarrass you by sniffing at people's bodies in the supermarket. If your child is like this, you might choose to ignore this section – though discriminatory meanings might distract him from bodies in a useful way.

Helping your child to think about tastes

Taste is a sense that is more difficult to talk about on its own than the other senses. This is partly because it's so mixed up with the idea of actually eating that we find it hard to separate it from how we feel about that. The child may associate the sense of taste with mealtime 'battles', and so may we; and for most of us this is the worst kind of battle, because as parents we probably feel that our biggest responsibility is to nourish our child properly.

As well as this, the sense of taste is mixed up with other senses. Obviously it's closely allied to *smell*, as we soon find if we lose our sense of smell with a head cold. But it's also affected by the *feel and texture* of food – for instance, a child may hate eggs or jelly or butter because the *feel* of them is disgusting to him; or he may eat anything crunchy, however it tastes, including earth or gravel! The *look* of food also affects how we perceive its taste, which is why good cooks take care to make food look appetizing in colour and form; children whose sight is poor, in fact, are very often difficult to feed because there is no visual interest in their food.

We do want our child to find mealtimes enjoyable (and we want to enjoy them too). We would also like him to accept a varied diet;

partly for his health, partly because it's much easier to live with children who aren't faddy, but also because we know that this could give him a lot of pleasure. Unfortunately, the 'resistance to change' that is such a feature of autism is often especially strong where foods are concerned; many eat only four or five different foods, and sometimes they will only eat one particular brand of each. Your child may also have certain diet restrictions that make variety difficult.

Within these restrictions, try to offer as wide a range of tastes as you can. For instance, does he regularly taste things in all the categories of sweet, salty, sour, bitter, bland? Do you make a game of trying out tiny tastes on his tongue as you cook, so that he learns about the flavour of ingredients separately? Do you only offer him tastes of sweet things, or do you try to make him adventurous by offering him a strong or unusual taste, on the tip of your finger maybe, when you've got something different out – anchovy, olives, strong cheese, crab? Even faddy children can surprise you.

What about cooking?

Unlike tired mums and dads, children usually like eating what they've made themselves, and cooking can be one of the most successful forms of play, even for children who don't play much in other ways. It offers many ways of experimenting with different concepts (eventually including shopping for ingredients and even, in time, reading).

Most parents, when they think about cooking with a child, think 'pastry'. This is not only a lot of trouble, but too difficult for many children. However, even young children with autism can often enjoy cooking if you choose something suitable and give them plenty of help. The satisfaction of making something that not only they, but the rest of the family, can eat with pleasure adds a new dimension to their play. If there are brothers and sisters, this may be a good activity to share with them, taking their abilities into account.

For instance, most children can stir up an instant whip and scatter chocolate dots on top, with help if necessary. Most, again with help, can put fillings on to ready-sliced and buttered bread for sandwiches. Many can mash or chop a banana, whip cream or dream topping with an electric whisk (hold their hand if they need this reassurance), and combine them. Or just get tubes of ready-made icing and make swirls on cake.

Again with help, little iced cakes made from a packet mix are really exciting to cook: an egg is stirred into the mix, which is spooned into the paper cases provided, and (after cooking) a water icing is mixed and spread, and decorations added, all from one packet. The skills the child learns from this are many – opening the packet, pouring out without spilling, pouring water bit by bit, stirring, spooning accurately, spreading, placing decorations – and of course you will later be able to use such activities to add measuring, counting, and even skilled egg-breaking, as well as all the talk that it can involve.

We've been cooking with children with autism, of different ages and abilities, for many years; and we love it because of all the opportunities we've listed here, because it can be organized to exactly suit the child's level, but most of all because the children themselves love it so much. The important thing in achieving this kind of success for younger or less able children is to have a helper for each child; you may need another adult if extra children are involved. And to see a hyperactive child with autism *carefully* decorating his instant whip and *slowly* carrying it to the table is a thrill for anyone who lives with a child who is contending with these problems. If you have a support group, try a cooking party that ends up as a feast.

SOME FINAL THOUGHTS ON PLAY

All through our discussions of play, we have emphasized the importance of the parent who plays *with* the child. He doesn't need your involvement in every single minute of his play, nor will he always want it; and you can't give all your attention to this one child. But he does need to be started off, and to be helped to keep going and move onward, much more than ordinary children.

The goals are the same for every child with autism: to plan his play in such a way that:

- he is enabled to enjoy the activity
- he learns to attend and cooperate long enough to carry him through to the 'pay-off', and therefore experiences success
- his play helps him to communicate with his parents, and other people
- he develops a little further his sense of mastering what may, for him, be a very confusing world.

And one enormous advantage most of us find, as we play alongside him, is that we become better and better at seeing things from his point of view. This more than anything will teach us ways of making play more rewarding to him, and therefore a richer learning experience.

USEFUL SOURCES OF INFORMATION

CHAPTER 1 – INTRODUCTION

Details of the action research project that led to the material in this book can be found in the following journal paper:

Chandler, S., Christie, P., Newson, E. and Prevezer, W. (2002) 'Developing a diagnostic and intervention package for 2- to 3-year-olds with autism. Outcomes of the Frameworks for Communication approach.' *Autism: The International Journal of Research and Practice 6*, 1, 47–69.

CHAPTER 5 – THE BEGINNINGS OF STRUCTURE

More information on the Makaton vocabulary and the symbols used is available from the Makaton website at:

www.makaton.org

CHAPTER 8 – MOVING TOWARDS SPOKEN LANGUAGE

More information on the Picture Exchange Communication System (PECS) approach to using symbols is available from the PECS website at:

www.pecs.org.uk

Caring for Myself

Christy Gast and Jane Krug

Photographs by Kotoe Laackman

Paperback, ISBN 978 1 84310 872 6, 96 pages

"This is a resource for young children that is certain to stand the practical tests of time and application! Simple and complete, parents and professionals will find themselves reaching for it time and again."

– Carol Gray, President, The Gray Center for Social Learning and Understanding and pioneer of Social Stories™

"With beautiful photos and simple, reassuring text, the authors and illustrator have created a remarkable resource. The step-by-step information will enable children to become familiar with basic routines so that they can approach them with both confidence and competence."

– Laurel A. Hoekman, Executive Director, The Gray Center for Social Learning and Understanding

"The information is clearly presented and sequenced so it makes sense to our children, pairing language with pictures. It also helps parents learn how to break down these tasks into smaller steps that can guide them as to how best to teach this information to their children."

– Michelle Garcia Winner, Center for Social Thinking, Inc

For a child with an autism spectrum disorder (ASD), even everyday activities like brushing your teeth, washing your hands or visiting the doctor can cause anxiety and stress because of the sensory, cognitive and communication impairments they experience.

Caring for Myself is an entertaining and educational social skills storybook that helps children with ASDs to understand the importance of taking care of their bodies. Fully illustrated with colour photographs, it sets out fun, simple steps that explain what caring for yourself actually involves – how you can do it, where it is done and why it is important. At the end of each story is a handy 'Pause for thought' page for parents which offers tips and strategies to help a child with each activity.

This charming book is much-loved by children with ASDs and enables them and their parents to cope with the daily activities that can be such a challenge.

Christy Gast is a publications and event co-ordinator for The Gray Center for Social Learning and Understanding with sixteen years' teaching experience. She is co-author of T*he Social Stories™ Quarterly*, and has two sons, one of whom has Asperger's Syndrome. She lives in Grand Rapids, Michigan. **Jane Krug** is a speech-language therapist, and has specialized in working with children with Autism Spectrum Disorder for nearly ten years. She volunteers her time at The Gray Center, lives in Ada, Michigan, and has a young daughter.

Fun with Messy Play
Ideas and Activities for Children with Special Needs
Tracey Beckerleg
Paperback, ISBN 978 1 84310 641 8, 160 pages

Messy play is a vital way for children to develop their sensory awareness of the world around them. *Fun with Messy Play* is an exciting activity book that stimulates the sensory perception of children with special needs through the imaginative use of everyday 'messy' materials, using activities such as fingering bowls of baked beans, walking through trays of paint and digging for treasure in a tub of jelly.

Tracey Beckerleg believes that these kinds of activities – not usually allowed in most homes and schools for being too messy – are exactly the kind of activities that young children with special needs should be engaging in. The vivid colours, squishy sounds, strange textures, tastes and smells engage the child in a stimulation of all senses, and do so without placing restrictive, stressful expectations on them.

This practical resource for parents and professionals shows how allowing children the freedom to play with sticky, gunky substances in an unashamedly messy way can not only stimulate sensory awareness but also improve their co-ordination, communicative and cognitive abilities, as well as boosting self-esteem and social skills.

Tracey Beckerleg has worked as a teacher for children with special needs for ten years, where she first began developing her approach to messy play. As a mother of five children, Tracey used messy play in her parenting. She lives in Hampshire, England, and is currently a home visitor for the National Portage Association, carrying out a home-visit educational service for pre-school children with support needs.

Enabling Communication in Children with Autism
Carol Potter and Chris Whittaker
Paperback, ISBN 978 1 85302 956 1, 208 pages

Addressing the complex issue of what constitutes a communication enabling environment for children with autism who use little or no speech, Potter and Whittaker show that the communication of these children can be significantly affected by a range of social and environmental influences. As well as providing an overview of the theoretical issues involved, Enabling Communication in Children with Autism provides detailed practical advice. Key elements of the recommended approach include

- the use of minimal speech
- proximal communication
- the use of appropriate systems of communication including multipointing
- providing many and varied opportunities for communication.

Arguing that encouraging spontaneous communication should be viewed as a major educational goal for these children, Potter and Whittaker demonstrate that these children can and do communicate in enabling environments and provide practical, proven strategies for creating such environments.

Carol Potter, BA(Hons), PGCE, M.Ed, has worked extensively in the field of autism as teacher, lecturer, consultant and researcher. She currently combines teaching with independent research and freelance staff training consultancy. **Chris Whittaker**, DAES, M.Ed, has taught, lectured and published in the field of special education for the last thirty years, with a particular interest in children with complex learning disabilities and autism. He is currently a Research Fellow at the University of Durham, and also works as a freelance consultant through CIRA-UK.

Playing, Laughing and Learning with Children on the Autism Spectrum
A Practical Resource of Play Ideas for Parents and Carers
Second Edition
Julia Moor
Paperback, ISBN 978 1 84310 6081, 304 pages

Praise for the first edition:

'An approachable and practical edition that will be welcomed by parents and carers alike. I know how hard it can be to find "How to" resources for parents. Well here is a gem.'

– *Children, Young People and Families*

Parents of young children newly diagnosed as on the autism spectrum are often at a loss for ideas about how best to help their child. *Playing, Laughing and Learning with Children on the Autism Spectrum* is not just a collection of play ideas; it shows how to break down activities into manageable stages, and looks at ways to gain a child's attention and motivation and to build on small achievements.

Each chapter covers a collection of ideas around a theme, including music, art, physical activities, playing outdoors, puzzles, turn-taking and using existing toys to create play sequences. There are also chapters on introducing reading and making the most of television. This updated second edition contains an extensive chapter on how to use the computer, the internet, and the digital camera to find and make resources and activities, and suggests many suitable websites to help parents through the internet maze. The ideas are useful both for toddlers and primary age children who are still struggling with play.

Julia Moor is a sensory art and communication tutor at a day service for adult learners and has worked for fourteen years with adults with multiple learning disabilities (including autism). She has a degree in psychology and is a qualified Further Education teacher. Her son Robin was diagnosed with autism at two; he is now a 'high functioning', bright and sociable eleven-year-old.

Helping Children with Complex Needs Bounce Back
Resilient Therapy ™ for Parents and Professionals
Kim Aumann and Angie Hart
Illustrated by Chloe Gerhardt
Paperback, ISBN 978 1 84310 948 8, 224 pages

'It is terrific to see a book for parents and professionals which shares knowledge and expertise on resilience – it is the key to parents and children getting through the tough times.'

– *Mary MacLeod, Chief Executive of the Family and Parenting Institute, UK*

'As a mother of four children, three of whom have a pick and mix of special needs including ADD, ADHD, Asperger's, high-functioning autism, anxiety and dyslexia – this book has been about building my own resilience as well as theirs. A boost in resilience is, I believe, what got my youngest through SATS, and building my resilience to deal with my ADHD son has improved our relationship enormously. The exercises were fun as well as informative. I think this book is really practical and positive.'

– *Karin Anjos, mother of four children with special needs*

'Caring for a disabled child with complex needs can be challenging for parents and for the professionals supporting them… This book offers a "magic box" of ideas, and a menu of coping strategies for families and those who support them. The emphasis is on practical steps forward, positive and achievable outcomes, with the end result of families feeling confident and competent in helping their own child to make progress.'

– *Dr Philippa Russell, Chair of Standing Commission on Carers, UK*

Resilient Therapy™ is an innovative way of strengthening children with complex needs. This is a tried-and-tested handbook for parents to read from cover to cover, or dip in and out of as needed. Accessible and fun, *Helping Children with Complex Needs Bounce Back* includes exercises and worksheets, as well as breaking down the principles of the latest research, making them easy to apply to everyday situations.

This 'magic box' of ideas and remedies is perfect for parents and carers, friends and families of children with disabilities, special educational needs, and mental or physical health needs, as well as professionals working with these children.

Kim Aumann is Director of ART (Amaze Research and Training). Amaze is a parent-led voluntary organization offering support and advice to parents of children with special needs and disabilities. She has been a practitioner in this area for 15 years. **Angie Hart** is Professor of Child, Family and Community Health at the University of Brighton. She is also the mother of three adopted children, all with special needs, and is a child and family therapist.

Art as an Early Intervention Tool for Children with Autism

Nicole Martin

Paperback, ISBN 978 1 84905 807 0, 160 pages

The early years are the most critical period of learning for a child with autism. Therapeutic art-making can be a useful tool to tap into their imaginations and help them to express their thoughts and feelings. *Art as an Early Intervention Tool for Children with Autism* includes practical advice on helping a child move beyond scribbling, organizing the child's environment for maximum comfort and relaxation, and providing physical and sensory support.

This book is packed with tips and suggestions for how to provide art therapy for children with autism — covering topics such as the basic materials required, safety issues, how to set up a workspace, and ideas for managing difficult behavior. The author writes from a professional and personal perspective — Nicole Martin is a qualified art therapist specializing in working with children with autism, and she also has a brother with autism.

Perfect for busy parents and as a practical reference for professionals such as psychologists, teachers, occupational therapists, sensory integration therapists and anyone working with a child on the autism spectrum.

Nicole Martin is a registered art therapist and licensed professional counselor, and big sister of a brother with autism. Nicole is the founder of Sky's the Limit Studio, which provides creative arts therapy services tailored to the needs of individuals with autism spectrum disorders.